The New Temple Shakespeare

Edited by M. R. RIDLEY, M.A.

TIMON
OF ATHENS

by William Shakespeare

J. M. DENT & SONS LTD., London
E. P. DUTTON & CO., INC., New York

Decorated by Eric Gill

First published in 1934

Published in this edition
by arrangement with E. P. Dutton & Co., Inc.,
201 Park Avenue South, New York, N.Y. 10003
and J. M. Dent & Sons Ltd.,
Bedford Street, London.

Editor's General Note

THE TEXT. The editor has kept before him the aim of presenting to the modern reader the nearest possible approximation to what Shakespeare actually wrote. The text is therefore conservative, and is based on the earliest reliable printed text. But to avoid distraction (*a*) the spelling is modernised, and (*b*) a limited number of universally accepted emendations is admitted without comment. Where a Quarto text exists as well as the First Folio the passages which occur only in the Quarto are enclosed in square brackets [ ] and those which occur only in the Folio in brace brackets { }.

SCENE DIVISION. The rapid continuity of the Elizabethan curtainless production is lost by the 'traditional' scene divisions. Where there is an essential difference of place these scene divisions are retained. Where on the other hand the change of place is insignificant the scene division is indicated only by a space on the page. For ease of reference, however, the 'traditional' division is retained at the head of the page and in line numbering.

NOTES. Passages on which there are notes are indicated by a † in the margin.

PUNCTUATION adheres more closely than has been usual to the 'Elizabethan' punctuation of the early texts. It is often therefore more indicative of the way in which the lines were to be delivered than of their syntactical construction.

GLOSSARIES are arranged on a somewhat novel principle, not alphabetically, but in the order in which the words or phrases occur. The editor is much indebted to Mr. J. N. Bryson for his collaboration in the preparation of the glossaries.

Preface

THE TEXT. The play was printed for the first time in the Folio of 1623. There is reason to suppose from the numbering of the pages that it took the place which had been originally intended for *Troilus and Cressida*. But whether there is any very real significance in this supposed substitution is more than doubtful. The text, if not 'the worst printed in the volume,' is certainly full of difficulties and at least apparent corruptions.

DATE OF COMPOSITION. For this there is no external evidence. Metrical tests place the play after *Hamlet*. The general tone of the play is that somewhat weary disillusionment, which yet has not the vigour to rise to tragedy, that one feels in *Troilus and Cressida*. And the author of it seems to have painfully in mind that problem of ingratitude which was in the mind of the author of *King Lear*.

THE AUTHORSHIP. The critics of this play have a sinister resemblance to the convocation of politic worms that set to work on the corpse of Polonius, though they are more eclectic in their tastes. They agree in one thing only, that the play is not the unaided or ungarbled or unmodified work of Shakespeare. Outside this general agreement, the permutations and combinations of the parts which are Shakespeare's, the parts which belong to an earlier play worked over by Shakespeare, the parts which he worked out in a rough draft and which were then completed by another hand, the parts which he never completed at all and had to be interpolated by another hand, the parts which are the result of an unskilful piecing together of actors' parts, and so on, and so on—their names are legion. All readers must feel reluctant to regard the play as we have it as a finished piece of Shakespeare's own work; but the evidence for the various theories whereby we can legitimately escape from the repugnant conclusion is much too extensive and too intricate to be given here in full, and it cannot be effectively summarised. Readers must be referred to (e.g.) Mr. K. Deighton's introduction to the 'Arden' edition of the play, where the evidence, such as it is, is very adequately presented by a refreshingly conservative editor, and in which a tribute, I think well justified, is paid to Verplanck. For the rest, there seems nothing to be done, for the purposes of this edition, but to give the play substantially as it appears in the First Folio; that is, in the shape in which, when all is said and done, Heminge and Condell chose to give it to the world as the work of their friend, with all its imperfections on its head.

SOURCES OF THE PLOT. In North's Plutarch, in the life of Antonius, there is a short account of Timon. Shakespeare could also have drawn upon Paynter's *Palace of Pleasure*, and, very particularly, if he could have arrived at it through the medium of a translation which does not appear to have existed, upon Lucian's dialogue, *Timon or the Misanthrope*. The apparent connection in many points between the play and the dialogue does strongly suggest that either Shakespeare had more Greek than he has been credited with, or that he was working over the production of an author who had read Lucian. It may be noticed that Timon had been in Shakespeare's mind as early as *L. L. L.*

CRITICISM. *Timon* is a savage play. There is an unrelieved bitterness about it unique in Shakespeare's work. It seems the work of a man not only preoccupied with the topic of ingratitude, as was perhaps the writer of *King Lear*, but also utterly disillusioned. With the exception of Flavius and Timon's servants there is not a character in it who does not merit Timon's disgust. If the world is made up of people like Timon's friends, like Alcibiades and his two whores, and like the professionally cynical Apemantus, if it is a world in which even the page catches the infection of the general rottenness, then we feel that we might as well become misanthropoi like Timon and hate mankind. One feels behind it something of that weary disgust with which Swift drew the Yahoos.

Hazlitt.[1]—Timon of Athens always appeared to us to be written with as intense a feeling of his subject as any one play of Shakespear. It is one of the few in which he seems to be in earnest throughout, never to trifle nor go out of his way. He does not relax in his efforts, nor lose sight of the unity of his design. It is the only play of our author

[1] Characters of Shakespear's Plays.

in which spleen is the predominant feeling of the mind. It is as much a satire as a play: and contains some of the finest pieces of invective possible to be conceived, both in the snarling captious answers of the cynic Apemantus, and in the impassioned and more terrible imprecations of Timon. The latter remind the classical reader of the force and swelling impetuosity of the moral declamations in *Juvenal*, while the former have all the keenness and caustic severity of the old Stoic philosophers. The soul of Diogenes appears to have been seated on the lips of Apemantus. The churlish profession of misanthropy in the cynic is contrasted with the profound feeling of it in Timon, and also with the soldier-like and determined resentment of Alcibiades against his countrymen, who have banished him.

Dowden.[1]—It would seem that about this period Shakspere's mind was much occupied with the questions, In what temper are we to receive the injuries inflicted upon us by our fellow men? How are we to bear ourselves towards those that wrong us? How shall we secure our inward being from chaos amid the evils of the world? How shall we attain to the most just and noble attitude of soul in which life and the injuries of life may be confronted? Now, here, in Timon we see one way in which a man may make his response to the injuries of life; he may turn upon the world with a fruitless and suicidal rage. Shakspere was interested in the history of Timon, not merely as a dramatic study, and not merely for the sake of moral edification, but because he recognised in the Athenian misanthrope one whom he had known, an intimate ac-

[1] Quoted from *Shakspere: His Mind and Art* by permission of the Publishers, Messrs. Kegan Paul, Trench, Trubner & Co., Ltd.

quaintance, the Timon of Shakspere's own breast. Shall we hesitate to admit that there was such a Timon in the breast of Shakspere? We are accustomed to speak of Shakspere's gentleness and Shakspere's tolerance so foolishly, that we find it easier to conceive of Shakspere as indulgent towards baseness and wickedness, than as feeling measureless rage and indignation against them—rage and indignation which would sometimes flash beyond their bounds, and strike at the whole wicked race of man. And it is certain that Shakspere's delight in human character, his quick and penetrating sympathy with almost every variety of man, saved him from any persistent injustice towards the world. But it can hardly be doubted, that the creator of Hamlet, of Lear, of Timon, saw clearly, and felt deeply, that there is a darker side to the world and to the soul of man.

THE LIFE OF
TIMON OF ATHENS

DRAMATIS PERSONÆ

TIMON, *a noble Athenian.*
LUCIUS,
LUCULLUS, } *flattering lords.*
SEMPRONIUS,
VENTIDIUS, *one of Timon's false friends.*
ALCIBIADES, *an Athenian captain.*
APEMANTUS, *a churlish philosopher.*
FLAVIUS, *steward to Timon.*
Poet, Painter, Jeweller, and Merchant.
An old Athenian.
FLAMINIUS,
LUCILIUS, } *servants to Timon.*
SERVILIUS,
CAPHIS,
PHILOTUS,
TITUS, } *servants to Timon's creditors*
HORTENSIUS, *and to the Lords.*
And others,
A Page. A Fool. Three Strangers.

PHRYNIA,
TIMANDRA, } *mistresses to Alcibiades.*

Cupid and Amazons in the mask.

Other Lords, Senators, Officers, Banditti, and Attendants.

SCENE: *Athens, and the neighbouring woods.*

THE LIFE OF
TIMON OF ATHENS

Act First

Athens. A hall in Timon's house

*Enter Poet, Painter, Jeweller, Merchant, and others,
at several doors*

Poet. Good day, sir.
Painter.　　　　　　I am glad you're well.
Poet. I have not seen you long; how goes the world?
Painter. It wears, sir, as it grows.
Poet.　　　　　　　　Ay, that's well known:
　But what particular rarity? what strange,
　Which manifold record not matches? See,
　Magic of bounty, all these spirits thy power
　Hath conjur'd to attend. I know the merchant.
Painter. I know them both: th' other's a jeweller.
Merchant. O, 'tis a worthy lord!
Jeweller.　　　　　　Nay, that's most fix'd.
Merchant. A most incomparable man, breath'd, as it
　　were,　　　　　　　　　　　　　　　　　10
　To an untirable and continuate goodness:
　He passes.
Jeweller. I have a jewel here—

1

Merchant. O, pray, let's see 't. For the Lord Timon,
    sir?

Jeweller. If he will touch the estimate. But for that—

Poet. (*reciting to himself*) 'When we for recom-
    pense have praised the vile,
    It stains the glory in that happy verse,
    Which aptly sings the good.'

Merchant. (*looking on the jewel*) 'Tis a good form.

Jeweller. And rich: here is a water, look ye.

Painter. You are rapt, sir, in some work, some
    dedication   20
    To the great lord.

Poet.   A thing slipp'd idly from me.
    Our poesy is as a gum, which oozes
    From whence 'tis nourish'd: the fire i' the flint
    Shows not, till it be struck: our gentle flame
    Provokes itself, and, like the current, flies
    Each bound it chafes. What have you there?

Painter. A picture, sir: when comes your book forth?

Poet. Upon the heels of my presentment, sir.
    Let's see your piece.

Painter. 'Tis a good piece.   30

Poet. So 'tis, this comes off well, and excellent.

Painter. Indifferent.

Poet.   Admirable: how this grace
    Speaks his own standing! what a mental power
    This eye shoots forth! how big imagination
    Moves in this lip, to the dumbness of the gesture,
    One might interpret.

Painter. It is a pretty mocking of the life:
    Here is a touch: is 't good?

Poet.   I will say of it,

It tutors nature, artificial strife
Lives in these touches, livelier than life.   40

Enter certain Senators, and pass over

Painter. How this lord is follow'd!
Poet. The senators of Athens, happy men!
Painter. Look, moe!
Poet. You see this confluence, this great flood of
    visitors,
  I have, in this rough work, shap'd out a man
  Whom this beneath world doth embrace and hug
  With amplest entertainment: my free drift
  Halts not particularly, but moves itself
  In a wide sea of wax, no levell'd malice   †
  Infects one comma in the course I hold,   50
  But flies an eagle flight, bold, and forth on,
  Leaving no tract behind.
Painter. How shall I understand you?
Poet.   I will unbolt to you.
  You see how all conditions, how all minds,
  As well of glib and slippery creatures as
  Of grave and austere quality, tender down
  Their services to Lord Timon: his large fortune,
  Upon his good and gracious nature hanging,
  Subdues and properties to his love and tendance
  All sorts of hearts; yea, from the glass-fac'd
    flatterer   60
  To Apemantus, that few things loves better
  Than to abhor himself; even he drops down
  The knee before him, and returns in peace
  Most rich in Timon's nod.
Painter.   I saw them speak together.

3

Poet. Sir, I have upon a high and pleasant hill
　Feign'd Fortune to be thron'd: the base o' the
　　mount
　Is rank'd with all deserts, all kind of natures
　That labour on the bosom of this sphere,
　To propagate their states; amongst them all,
　Whose eyes are on this sovereign lady fix'd,　　　　70
　One do I personate of Lord Timon's frame,
　Whom Fortune with her ivory hand wafts to her,
　Whose present grace to present slaves and
　　servants
　Translates his rivals.
Painter.　　　　　　'Tis conceiv'd to scope.
　This throne, this Fortune, and this hill, methinks,
　With one man beckon'd from the rest below,
　Bowing his head against the steepy mount
　To climb his happiness, would be well express'd
　In our condition.
Poet.　　　　　　Ay, sir, but hear me on:
　All those which were his fellows but of late,　　　　80
　Some better than his value, on the moment
　Follow his strides, his lobbies fill with tendance,
　Rain sacrificial whisperings in his ear,
　Make sacred even his stirrup, and through him
　Drink the free air.
Painter.　　　　　Ay, marry, what of these!
Poet. When Fortune in her shift and change of
　　mood
　Spurns down her late belov'd, all his dependants
　Which labour'd after him to the mountain's top
　Even on their knees and hands, let him sit down,　　†
　Not one accompanying his declining foot.　　　　　90

4

Painter. 'Tis common:
A thousand moral paintings I can show,
That shall demonstrate these quick blows of
    Fortune's,
More pregnantly than words. Yet you do well,
To show Lord Timon that mean eyes have seen
The foot above the head.

*Trumpets sound. Enter Lord Timon, addressing himself
courteously to every suitor; a Messenger from Ventidius
talking with him; Lucilius and other servants following*

Timon.   Imprison'd is he, say you?
Messenger. Ay, my good lord, five talents is his debt;
His means most short, his creditors most strait:
Your honourable letter he desires
To those have shut him up, which failing,   100
Periods his comfort.
Timon.   Noble Ventidius, well:
I am not of that feather to shake off
My friend when he must need me. I do know him
A gentleman that well deserves a help,
Which he shall have. I'll pay the debt, and free
    him.
Messenger. Your lordship ever binds him.
Timon. Commend me to him, I will send his ransom,
And, being enfranchis'd, bid him come to me;
'Tis not enough to help the feeble up,
But to support him after. Fare you well.   110
Messenger. All happiness to your honour!   *Exit*

Enter an old Athenian

Athenian. Lord Timon, hear me speak.

Timon.   Freely, good father.
Athenian. Thou hast a servant nam'd Lucilius.
Timon. I have so: what of him?
Athenian. Most noble Timon, call the man before
    thee.
Timon. Attends he here, or no? Lucilius!
Lucilius. Here at your lordship's service.
Athenian. This fellow here, Lord Timon, this thy
    creature,
  By night frequents my house. I am a man
  That from my first have been inclin'd to thrift,   120
  And my estate deserves an heir more rais'd
  Than one which holds a trencher.
Timon.   Well: what further?
Athenian. One only daughter have I, no kin else,
  On whom I may confer what I have got:
  The maid is fair, o' the youngest for a bride,
  And I have bred her at my dearest cost
  In qualities of the best. This man of thine
  Attempts her love: I prithee, noble lord,
  Join with me to forbid him her resort,
  Myself have spoke in vain.
Timon.   The man is honest.   130
Athenian. Therefore he will be Timon,   †
  His honesty rewards him in itself;
  It must not bear my daughter.
Timon.   Does she love him?
Athenian. She is young and apt:
  Our own precedent passions do instruct us
  What levity's in youth.
Timon. (to Lucilius)   Love you the maid?
Lucilius. Ay, my good lord, and she accepts of it.

6

Athenian. If in her marriage my consent be missing,
  I call the gods to witness, I will choose
  Mine heir from forth the beggars of the world,   140
  And dispossess her all.
Timon.   How shall she be endow'd
  If she be mated with an equal husband?
Athenian. Three talents on the present; in future,
  all.
Timon. This gentleman of mine hath serv'd me long:
  To build his fortune, I will strain a little,
  For 'tis a bond in men. Give him thy daughter,
  What you bestow, in him I'll counterpoise,
  And make him weigh with her.
Athenian.   Most noble lord,
  Pawn me to this your honour, she is his.
Timon. My hand to thee, mine honour on my
  promise.   150
Lucilius. Humbly I thank your lordship: never may
  That state or fortune fall into my keeping,
  Which is not ow'd to you!
          Exeunt Lucilius and Old Athenian
Poet. Vouchsafe my labour, and long live your lord-
  ship!
Timon. I thank you, you shall hear from me anon:
  Go not away. What have you there, my friend?
Painter. A piece of painting, which I do beseech
  Your lordship to accept.
Timon.   Painting is welcome.
  The painting is almost the natural man;
  For since dishonour traffics with man's nature,   160
  He is but outside: these pencill'd figures are
  Even such as they give out. I like your work,

And you shall find I like it; wait attendance
Till you hear further from me.
Painter.　　　　　　　　The gods preserve ye!
Timon. Well fare you, gentleman: give me your
　　hand.
We must needs dine together: sir, your jewel
Hath suffer'd under praise.
Jeweller.　　　　　　What, my lord, dispraise?
Timon. A mere satiety of commendations.
If I should pay you for 't as 'tis extoll'd,
It would unclew me quite.
Jeweller.　　　　　　　My lord, 'tis rated　　170
As those which sell would give: but you well
　　know,
Things of like value, differing in the owners,
Are prized by their masters. Believe 't, dear lord,
You mend the jewel by the wearing it.
Timon. Well mock'd.
Merchant. No, my good lord, he speaks the common
　　tongue,
Which all men speak with him.
Timon. Look who comes here, will you be chid?

Enter Apemantus

Jeweller. We'll bear with your lordship.
Merchant.　　　　　　　　He'll spare none.
Timon. Good morrow to thee, gentle Apemantus!　180
Apemantus. Till I be gentle, stay thou for thy good
　　morrow.
When thou art Timon's dog, and these knaves
　　honest.

Timon. Why dost thou call them knaves? thou
know'st them not.

Apemantus. Are they not Athenians?

Timon. Yes.

Apemantus. Then I repent not.

Jeweller. You know me, Apemantus?

Apemantus. Thou know'st I do, I call'd thee by thy
name.

Timon. Thou art proud, Apemantus?   190

Apemantus. Of nothing so much as that I am not
like Timon.

Timon. Whither art going?

Apemantus. To knock out an honest Athenian's
brains.

Timon. That's a deed thou'lt die for.

Apemantus. Right, if doing nothing be death by the
law.

Timon. How lik'st thou this picture, Apemantus?

Apemantus. The best, for the innocence.   200

Timon. Wrought he not well that painted it?

Apemantus. He wrought better that made the
painter, and yet he's but a filthy piece of work.

Painter. You're a dog.

Apemantus. Thy mother's of my generation: what's
she, if I be a dog?

Timon. Wilt dine with me, Apemantus?

Apemantus. No: I eat not lords.

Timon. An thou shouldst, thou'ldst anger ladies.

Apemantus. O, they eat lords; so they come by great   210
bellies.

Timon. That's a lascivious apprehension.

9

Apemantus. So, thou apprehend'st it, take it for thy
labour.

Timon. How dost thou like this jewel, Apemantus?

Apemantus. Not so well as plain-dealing, which will
not cost a man a doit.

Timon. What dost thou think 'tis worth?

Apemantus. Not worth my thinking. How now,
poet?   220

Poet. How now, philosopher?

Apemantus. Thou liest.

Poet. Art not one?

Apemantus. Yes.

Poet. Then I lie not.

Apemantus. Art not a poet?

Poet. Yes.

Apemantus. Then thou liest: look in thy last work,
where thou hast feign'd him a worthy fellow.

Poet. That's not feign'd, he is so.   230

Apemantus. Yes, he is worthy of thee, and to pay
thee for thy labour. He that loves to be flatter'd
is worthy o' the flatterer. Heavens, that I were a
lord!

Timon. What wouldst do then, Apemantus?

Apemantus. E'en as Apemantus does now, hate a
lord with my heart.

Timon. What, thyself?

Apemantus. Ay.

Timon. Wherefore?   240

Apemantus. That I had no angry wit to be a lord.   †
Art not thou a merchant?

Merchant. Ay, Apemantus.

10

1

Apemantus. Traffic confound thee, if the gods will
　　not!
Merchant. If traffic do it, the gods do it.
Apemantus. Traffic's thy god, and thy god con-
　　found thee!

Trumpet sounds. Enter a Messenger

Timon. What trumpet's that?
Messenger. 'Tis Alcibiades, and some twenty horse　　250
　　All of companionship.
Timon. Pray entertain them, give them guide to us.
　　　　　　　　　Exeunt some Attendants
　　You must needs dine with me: go not you hence
　　Till I have thank'd you: when dinner's done,
　　Show me this piece. I am joyful of your sights.

Enter Alcibiades, with the rest

　　Most welcome, sir!
Apemantus. 　　　So, so, there!
　　Aches contract and starve your supple joints!
　　That there should be small love 'mongst these
　　　　sweet knaves,
　　And all this courtesy! The strain of man's bred
　　　　out
　　Into baboon and monkey.　　　　　　　　　　260
Alcibiades. Sir, you have sav'd my longing, and I
　　　　feed
　　Most hungerly on your sight.
Timon. 　　　　　　　Right welcome, sir!
　　Ere we depart, we'll share a bounteous time
　　In different pleasures. Pray you, let us in.
　　　　　　　　　Exeunt all but Apemantus

2

Enter two Lords

First Lord. What time o' day is 't, Apemantus?

Apemantus. Time to be honest.

First Lord. That time serves still.

Apemantus. The most accursed thou, that still omitt'st it.

Sec. Lord. Thou art going to Lord Timon's feast?

Apemantus. Ay, to see meat fill knaves, and wine heat fools.   270

Sec. Lord. Fare thee well, fare thee well.

Apemantus. Thou art a fool to bid me farewell twice.

Sec. Lord. Why, Apemantus?

Apemantus. Shouldst have kept one to thyself, for I mean to give thee none.

First Lord. Hang thyself!

Apemantus. No, I will do nothing at thy bidding: make thy requests to thy friend.

Sec. Lord. Away, unpeaceable dog, or I'll spurn thee hence!   280

Apemantus. I will fly, like a dog, the heels o' the ass.

Exit

First Lord. He's opposite to humanity. Come, shall we in,

And taste Lord Timon's bounty? he outgoes
The very heart of kindness.

Sec. Lord. He pours it out: Plutus, the god of gold,
Is but his steward: no meed but he repays
Sevenfold above itself: no gift to him,
But breeds the giver a return, exceeding
All use of quittance.

First Lord.   The noblest mind he carries
   That ever govern'd man.   290
Sec. Lord. Long may he live in fortunes! Shall we
      in?
   I'll keep you company.   *Exeunt*

*Hautboys playing loud music. A great banquet served in;
Flavius and others attending; and then enter Lord Timon,
Alcibiades, Lords, Senators, and Ventidius. Then comes,
dropping after all, Apemantus, discontentedly, like himself.*

Ventidius. Most honour'd Timon,
   It hath pleas'd the gods to remember my father's
      age,
   And call him to long peace:
   He is gone happy, and has left me rich:
   Then, as in grateful virtue I am bound
   To your free heart, I do return those talents,
   Doubled with thanks and service, from whose
      help
   I deriv'd liberty.
Timon.   O, by no means,
   Honest Ventidius; you mistake my love,
   I gave it freely ever, and there's none   10
   Can truly say he gives, if he receives:
   If our betters play at that game, we must not dare
   To imitate them; faults that are rich are fair.
Ventidius. A noble spirit!

13

Timon. Nay, my lords, ceremony was but devis'd at
    first
    To set a gloss on faint deeds, hollow welcomes,
    Recanting goodness, sorry ere 'tis shown:
    But where there is true friendship, there needs
      none.
    Pray, sit; more welcome are ye to my fortunes
    Than my fortunes to me.   *They sit*   20
First Lord. My lord, we always have confess'd it.
Apemantus. Ho, ho, confess'd it? hang'd it, have you
    not?
Timon. O, Apemantus, you are welcome.
Apemantus.   No:
    You shall not make me welcome:
    I come to have thee thrust me out of doors.
Timon. Fie, thou'rt a churl, ye've got a humour
    there
    Does not become a man; 'tis much to blame.
    They say, my lords, '*ira furor brevis est*;' but yond
    man is ever angry. Go, let him have a table by
    himself; for he does neither affect company, nor   30
    is he fit for 't indeed.
Apemantus. Let me stay at thine apperil, Timon:
    I come to observe; I give thee warning on 't.
Timon. I take no heed of thee: thou'rt an Athenian,
    therefore welcome: I myself would have no
    power, prithee, let my meat make thee silent.
Apemantus. I scorn thy meat, 'twould choke me:
    for I should ne'er flatter thee. O you gods, what
    a number of men eats Timon, and he sees 'em
    not! It grieves me to see so many dip their meat   40

in one man's blood, and all the madness is, he
cheers them up too.
I wonder men dare trust themselves with men:
Methinks they should invite them without knives,
Good for their meat, and safer for their lives.
There's much example for 't; the fellow that sits
next him, now parts bread with him, pledges the
breath of him in a divided draught, is the readiest
man to kill him: 't has been prov'd. If I were a
huge man, I should fear to drink at meals. 50
Lest they should spy my windpipe's dangerous
    notes: †
Great men should drink with harness on their
    throats.

Timon. My lord, in heart; and let the health go
    round.

Sec. Lord. Let it flow this way, my good lord.

Apemantus. Flow this way? A brave fellow! he
keeps his tides well; those healths will make thee
and thy state look ill, Timon. Here's that which is
too weak to be a sinner, honest water, which ne'er
left man i' the mire:
This and my food are equals; there's no odds: 60
Feasts are too proud to give thanks to the gods.
                Apemantus's Grace
        Immortal gods, I crave no pelf,
        I pray for no man but myself,
        Grant I may never prove so fond,
        To trust man on his oath or bond:
        Or a harlot for her weeping,
        Or a dog that seems a-sleeping,
        Or a keeper with my freedom,

15

Or my friends, if I should need 'em.
Amen. So fall to 't: 70
Rich men sin, and I eat root.

Eats and drinks

Much good dich thy good heart, Apemantus!

Timon. Captain Alcibiades, your heart's in the field
now.

Alcibiades. My heart is ever at your service, my
lord.

Timon. You had rather be at a breakfast of enemies
than a dinner of friends.

Alcibiades. So they were bleeding-new, my lord,
there's no meat like 'em; I could wish my best   80
friend at such a feast.

Apemantus. Would all those flatterers were thine
enemies, then, that then thou mightst kill 'em;
and bid me to 'em!

First Lord. Might we but have that happiness, my
lord, that you would once use our hearts, whereby we might express some part of our zeals, we
should think ourselves for ever perfect.

Timon. O, no doubt, my good friends, but the gods
themselves have provided that I shall have much   90
help from you: how had you been my friends
else? why have you that charitable title from
thousands? Did not you chiefly belong to my
heart? I have told more of you to myself than
you can with modesty speak in your own behalf.
And thus far I confirm you. O you gods (think I)
what need we have any friends, if we should ne'er
have need of 'em? they were the most needless
creatures living, should we ne'er have use for

'em; and would most resemble sweet instruments   100
hung up in cases, that keeps their sounds to themselves. Why, I have often wished myself poorer,
that I might come nearer to you. We are born to
do benefits: and what better or properer can we
call our own than the riches of our friends? O,
what a precious comfort 'tis, to have so many
like brothers commanding one another's fortunes! O joy's e'en made away ere 't can be born!
Mine eyes cannot hold out water, methinks: to
forget their faults, I drink to you.   110

Apemantus. Thou weep'st to make them drink,
Timon.

Sec. Lord. Joy had the like conception in our eyes,
And at that instant like a babe sprung up.

Apemantus. Ho, ho! I laugh to think that babe a
bastard.

Third Lord. I promise you, my lord, you mov'd
me much.

Apemantus. Much!   *Tucket, within*

Timon. What means that trump?

Enter a Servant

How now?

Servant. Please you, my lord, there are certain ladies
most desirous of admittance.   120

Timon. Ladies? what are their wills?

Servant. There comes with them a forerunner, my
lord, which bears that office, to signify their
pleasures.

Timon. I pray, let them be admitted.

17

Enter Cupid

Cupid. Hail to thee, worthy Timon, and to all
   That of his bounties taste! The five best senses
   Acknowledge thee their patron, and come freely
   To gratulate thy plenteous bosom:
   Th' ear, taste, touch, smell, pleas'd from thy table
     rise;   130
   They only now come but to feast thine eyes.
Timon. They're welcome all, let 'em have kind ad-
     mittance.
   Music make their welcome!   *Exit Cupid*
First Lord. You see, my lord, how ample you're
     belov'd.

Music. Re-enter Cupid, with a mask of Ladies as Amazons,
with lutes in their hands, dancing and playing

Apemantus. Hoy-day, what a sweep of vanity comes
     this way!
   They dance! they are mad women.
   Like madness is the glory of this life,   †
   As this pomp shows to a little oil and root.
   We make ourselves fools, to disport ourselves,
   And spend our flatteries, to drink those men   140
   Upon whose age we void it up again
   With poisonous spite and envy.
   Who lives, that's not depraved or depraves?
   Who dies, that bears not one spurn to their graves
   Of their friends' gift?
   I should fear, those that dance before me now
   Would one day stamp upon me: 't has been done;
   Men shut their doors against a setting sun.

*The Lords rise from table, with much adoring of Timon
and to show their loves, each singles out an Amazon, and
all dance, men with women, a lofty strain or two to the
hautboys, and cease*

Timon. You have done our pleasures much grace,
    fair ladies,
Set a fair fashion on our entertainment,   150
Which was not half so beautiful and kind:
You have added worth unto 't, and lustre,
And entertain'd me with mine own device.
I am to thank you for 't.
First Lady. My lord, you take us even at the best.
Apemantus. Faith, for the worst is filthy, and would
    not hold taking, I doubt me.
Timon. Ladies, there is an idle banquet attends you,
    Please you to dispose yourselves.
All Ladies. Most thankfully, my lord.   160
               Exeunt Cupid and Ladies
Timon. Flavius!
Flavius. My lord?
Timon.   The little casket bring me hither.
Flavius. Yes, my lord. (*aside*) More jewels yet?
    There is no crossing him in 's humour,
    Else I should tell him well, i' faith I should;
    When all's spent, he'ld be cross'd then, an he
      could:
    'Tis pity bounty had not eyes behind,
    That man might ne'er be wretched for his mind.
                        Exit
First Lord. Where be our men?
Servant. Here, my lord, in readiness.   170
Sec. Lord. Our horses!

Re-enter Flavius, with the casket

Timon. O my friends,
   I have one word to say to you: look you, my good
     lord,
   I must entreat you honour me so much
   As to advance this jewel, accept it, and wear it,
   Kind my lord.
First Lord. I am so far already in your gifts,—
All. So are we all.

Enter a Servant

Servant. My lord, there are certain nobles of the
   senate newly alighted, and come to visit you.   180
Timon. They are fairly welcome.
Flavius. I beseech your honour, vouchsafe me a
   word; it does concern you near.
Timon. Near? why then another time I'll hear thee.
   I prithee, let's be provided to show them enter-
   tainment.
Flavius. (*aside*) I scarce know how.

Enter another Servant

Sec. Serv. May it please your honour, Lord Lucius
   (Out of his free love) hath presented to you
   Four milk-white horses, trapp'd in silver.
Timon. I shall accept them fairly: let the presents   190
   Be worthily entertain'd.

Enter a third Servant

                  How now? what news?
Third Serv. Please you, my lord, that honourable
   gentleman, Lord Lucullus, entreats your com-

pany to-morrow, to hunt with him, and has sent
your honour two brace of greyhounds.
Timon. I'll hunt with him, and let them be receiv'd,
Not without fair reward.
Flavius.   (*aside*) What will this come to?
He commands us to provide, and give great gifts,
And all out of an empty coffer:
Nor will he know his purse, or yield me this,   200
To show him what a beggar his heart is,
Being of no power to make his wishes good.
His promises fly so beyond his state,
That what he speaks is all in debt, he owes
For every word; he is so kind that he now
Pays interest for 't; his land's put to their books.
Well, would I were gently put out of office,
Before I were forc'd out!
Happier is he that has no friend to feed,
Than such that do e'en enemies exceed.   210
I bleed inwardly for my lord.   *Exit*
Timon.   You do yourselves
Much wrong, you bate too much of your own
    merits.
Here, my lord, a trifle of our love.
Sec. Lord. With more than common thanks I will
    receive it.
Third Lord. O, he's the very soul of bounty!
Timon. And now I remember, my lord, you gave
good words the other day of a bay courser I rode
on. 'Tis yours because you lik'd it.
Third Lord. O, I beseech you, pardon me, my lord,
    in that.

Timon. You may take my word, my lord; I know
   no man   220
  Can justly praise but what he does affect:
  I weigh my friend's affection with mine own:
  I'll tell you true. I'll call to you.
All Lords. O, none so welcome.
Timon. I take all and your several visitations
  So kind to heart, 'tis not enough to give:
  Methinks, I could deal kingdoms to my friends,
  And ne'er be weary. Alcibiades,
  Thou art a soldier, therefore seldom rich,
  It comes in charity to thee: for all thy living   230
  Is 'mongst the dead; and all the lands thou hast
  Lie in a pitch'd field.
Alcibiades. Ay, defil'd land, my lord.
First Lord. We are so virtuously bound—
Timon.   And so
  Am I to you.
Sec. Lord. So infinitely endear'd—
Timon. All to you. Lights, more lights!
First Lord. The best of happiness,
  Honour, and fortunes, keep with you, Lord
  Timon!
Timon. Ready for his friends.
               Exeunt all but Apemantus and Timon
Apemantus.   What a coil's here! 240
  Serving of becks and jutting-out of bums!
  I doubt whether their legs be worth the sums
  That are given for 'em. Friendship's full of dregs:
  Methinks false hearts should never have sound
    legs.

Thus honest fools lay out their wealth on court'sies.

Timon. Now, Apemantus (if thou wert not sullen) I would be good to thee.

Apemantus. No, I'll nothing: for if I should be brib'd too, there would be none left to rail upon thee, and then thou wouldst sin the faster. Thou giv'st so long, Timon (I fear me) thou wilt give away thyself in paper shortly. What needs these feasts, pomps and vain-glories?

Timon. Nay, an you begin to rail on society once, I am sworn not to give regard to you. Farewell, and come with better music. *Exit*

Apemantus. So: thou wilt not hear me now, thou shalt not then. I'll lock thy heaven from thee:
O, that men's ears should be
To counsel deaf, but not to flattery! *Exit* 260

250

†

Act Second

SCENE I

A Senator's house

Enter a Senator, with papers in his hand

Senator. And late five thousand: to Varro and to Isidore
He owes nine thousand, besides my former sum,
Which makes it five and twenty. Still in motion

23

Of raging waste? It cannot hold, it will not.
If I want gold, steal but a beggar's dog
And give it Timon, why, the dog coins gold.
If I would sell my horse, and buy twenty moe
Better than he, why, give my horse to Timon;
Ask nothing, give it him, it foals me straight
And able horses: no porter at his gate,   †
But rather one that smiles, and still invites   11
All that pass by. It cannot hold, no reason
Can found his state in safety. Caphis, ho!
Caphis, I say!

Enter Caphis

Caphis.   Here, sir; what is your pleasure?
Senator. Get on your cloak, and haste you to Lord
    Timon,
Importune him for my moneys, be not ceas'd
With slight denial; nor then silenc'd, when—
'Commend me to your master'—and the cap
Plays in the right hand, thus: but tell him,
My uses cry to me; I must serve my turn   20
Out of mine own, his days and times are past,
And my reliances on his fracted dates
Have smit my credit. I love, and honour him,
But must not break my back to heal his finger.
Immediate are my needs, and my relief
Must not be toss'd and turn'd to me in words,
But find supply immediate. Get you gone,
Put on a most importunate aspect,
A visage of demand; for I do fear
When every feather sticks in his own wing,   30
Lord Timon will be left a naked gull,

Which flashes now a phœnix; get you gone.
Caphis. I go, sir.
Senator. Ay, go, sir! Take the bonds along with you,
  And have the dates in. Come.
Caphis.   I will, sir.
Senator.   Go.

                              Exeunt

SCENE II

A hall in Timon's house

Enter Flavius, with many bills in his hand

Flavius. No care, no stop, so senseless of expense,
  That he will neither know how to maintain it,
  Nor cease his flow of riot. Takes no account
  How things go from him, nor resumes no care
  Of what is to continue: never mind
  Was to be so unwise, to be so kind.
  What shall be done, he will not hear, till feel:
  I must be round with him, now he comes from
    hunting.
  Fie, fie, fie, fie!

Enter Caphis, with the Servants of Isidore and Varro

Caphis. Good even, Varro: what, you come for
    money?   10
Var. Serv. Is 't not your business too?
Caphis. It is, and yours too, Isidore?
Isid. Serv. It is so.
Caphis. Would we were all discharg'd!
Var. Serv. I fear it.

25

Caphis. Here comes the lord.

Enter Timon, Alcibiades, Lords, and others

Timon. So soon as dinner's done, we'll forth again,
   My Alcibiades. With me? what is your will?
Caphis. My lord, here is a note of certain dues.
Timon. Dues? Whence are you?
Caphis.   Of Athens here, my lord.   20
Timon. Go to my steward.
Caphis. Please it your lordship, he hath put me off
   To the succession of new days this month:
   My master is awak'd by great occasion
   To call upon his own, and humbly prays you
   That with your other noble parts you'll suit,
   In giving him his right.
Timon.   Mine honest friend,
   I prithee but repair to me next morning.
Caphis. Nay, good my lord,—
Timon.   Contain thyself, good friend.
Var. Serv. One Varro's servant, my good lord,—   30
Isid. Serv. From Isidore; he humbly prays your
   speedy payment.
Caphis. If you did know, my lord, my master's
   wants,—
Var. Serv. 'Twas due on forfeiture, my lord, six
   weeks, and past.
Isid. Serv. Your steward puts me off, my lord, and I
   Am sent expressly to your lordship.
Timon. Give me breath.
   I do beseech you, good my lords, keep on,
   I'll wait upon you instantly.
                    Exeunt Alcibiades, Lords, &c.

        (*to Flavius*) Come hither: pray you,   40
How goes the world, that I am thus encounter'd
With clamorous demands of debt, broken bonds,
And the detention of long-since-due debts,
Against my honour?
Flavius.   Please you, gentlemen,
The time is unagreeable to this business:
Your importunacy cease, till after dinner,
That I may make his lordship understand
Wherefore you are not paid.
Timon. Do so my friends; see them well en-
    tertain'd.   *Exit*
Flavius. Pray, draw near.   *Exit*   50

            Enter Apemantus and Fool

Caphis. Stay, stay, here comes the fool with Ape-
    mantus, let's ha' some sport with 'em.
Var. Serv. Hang him, he'll abuse us.
Isid. Serv. A plague upon him, dog!
Var. Serv. How dost, fool?
Apemantus. Dost dialogue with thy shadow?
Var. Serv. I speak not to thee.
Apemantus. No, 'tis to thyself. (*to the Fool*) Come
    away.
Isid. Serv. There's the fool hangs on your back   60
    already.
Apemantus. No, thou stand'st single, thou'rt not on
    him yet.
Caphis. Where's the fool now?
Apemantus. He last ask'd the question. Poor rogues,
    and usurers' men, bawds between gold and want!

27

All Serv. What are we, Apemantus?

Apemantus. Asses.

All Serv. Why?

Apemantus. That you asked me what you are, and   70
do not know yourselves. Speak to 'em, fool.

Fool. How do you, gentlemen?

All Serv. Gramercies, good fool: how does your
mistress?

Fool. She's e'en setting on water to scald such
chickens as you are. Would we could see you at
Corinth!

Apemantus. Good! gramercy.

Enter Page

Fool. Look you, here comes my master's page.

Page (to the Fool) Why, how now, captain? what   80
do you in this wise company? How dost thou,
Apemantus?

Apemantus. Would I had a rod in my mouth, that
I might answer thee profitably.

Page. Prithee, Apemantus, read me the superscrip-
tion of these letters, I know not which is which.

Apemantus. Canst not read?

Page. No.

Apemantus. There will little learning die then, that
day thou art hang'd. This is to Lord Timon, this   90
to Alcibiades. Go; thou wast born a bastard, and
and thou'lt die a bawd.

Page. Thou wast whelp'd a dog, and thou shalt
famish a dog's death. Answer not, I am gone.

Exit

28

Apemantus. E'en so thou outrun'st grace; fool, I will
　　go with you to Lord Timon's.

Fool. Will you leave me there?

Apemantus. If Timon stay at home. You three serve
　　three usurers?

All Serv. I would they serv'd us!　　　　　　　　　100

Apemantus. So would I,—as good a trick as ever
　　hangman serv'd thief.

Fool. Are you three usurers' men?

All Serv. Ay, fool.

Fool. I think no usurer but has a fool to his servant.
　　My mistress is one, and I am her fool: when men
　　come to borrow of your masters, they approach
　　sadly, and go away merry; but they enter my
　　master's house merrily, and go away sadly. The　110
　　reason of this?

Var. Serv. I could render one.

Apemantus. Do it then, that we may account thee
　　a whoremaster, and a knave, which notwith-
　　standing thou shalt be no less esteem'd.

Var. Serv. What is a whoremaster, fool?

Fool. A fool in good clothes, and something like
　　thee. 'Tis a spirit, sometime 't appears like a lord,
　　sometime like a lawyer, sometime like a philoso-
　　pher, with two stones moe than's artificial one.　120
　　He is very often like a knight; and generally, in
　　all shapes that man goes up and down in, from
　　fourscore to thirteen, this spirit walks in.

Var. Serv. Thou art not altogether a fool.

Fool. Nor thou altogether a wise man; as much
　　foolery as I have, so much wit thou lack'st.

Apemantus. That answer might have become
  Apemantus.
All Serv. Aside, aside, here comes Lord Timon.

Re-enter Timon and Flavius

Apemantus. Come with me, fool, come.   130
Fool. I do not always follow lover, elder brother,
  and woman; sometime the philosopher.
Exeunt Apemantus and Fool
Flavius. Pray you, walk near, I'll speak with you
  anon.
Exeunt Servants
Timon. You make me marvel wherefore, ere this
    time,
  Had you not fully laid my state before me,
  That I might so have rated my expense
  As I had leave of means.
Flavius.   You would not hear me
  At many leisures I propos'd.
Timon.   Go to:
  Perchance some single vantages you took,
  When my indisposition put you back,   140
  And that unaptness made your minister,
  Thus to excuse yourself.
Flavius.   O my good lord,
  At many times I brought in my accounts,
  Laid them before you, you would throw them off,
  And say, you found them in mine honesty;
  When for some trifling present you have bid me
  Return so much, I have shook my head, and
    wept:
  Yea, 'gainst the authority of manners, pray'd you

30

To hold your hand more close: I did endure
Not seldom, nor no slight checks, when I have   150
Prompted you in the ebb of your estate,
And your great flow of debts; my lov'd lord,
Though you hear now (too late) yet now's a
   time
The greatest of your having lacks a half
To pay your present debts.
Timon.   Let all my land be sold.
Flavius. 'Tis all engag'd, some forfeited and gone,
And what remains will hardly stop the mouth
Of present dues; the future comes apace:
What shall defend the interim? and at length
How goes our reckoning?   160
Timon. To Lacedæmon did my land extend.
Flavius. O my good lord, the world is but a word,
Were it all yours, to give it in a breath,
How quickly were it gone!
Timon.   You tell me true.
Flavius. If you suspect my husbandry or falsehood,
Call me before the exactest auditors,
And set me on the proof. So the gods bless me,
When all our offices have been oppress'd
With riotous feeders, when our vaults have wept
With drunken spilth of wine; when every room   170
Hath blaz'd with lights, and bray'd with min-
   strelsy,
I have retir'd me to a wasteful cock,   †
And set mine eyes at flow.
Timon.   Prithee, no more.
Flavius. Heavens, have I said, the bounty of this
   lord!

31

How many prodigal bits have slaves and peasants
This night englutted! Who is not Timon's?
What heart, head, sword, force, means, but is
    Lord Timon's?
Great Timon, noble, worthy, royal Timon!
Ah, when the means are gone, that buy this
    praise,
The breath is gone whereof this praise is made: 180
Feast-won, fast-lost; one cloud of winter showers,
These flies are couch'd.
Timon.   Come, sermon me no further.
No villanous bounty yet hath pass'd my heart;
Unwisely, not ignobly, have I given.
Why dost thou weep, canst thou the conscience
    lack,
To think I shall lack friends? Secure thy heart;
If I would broach the vessels of my love,
And try the argument of hearts, by borrowing,
Men, and men's fortunes could I frankly use
As I can bid thee speak.
Flavius.   Assurance bless your thoughts!   190
Timon. And in some sort these wants of mine are
    crown'd,
That I account them blessings. For by these
Shall I try friends. You shall perceive how you
Mistake my fortunes; I am wealthy in my friends.
Within there! Flaminius! Servilius!

Enter Flaminius, Servilius, and other Servants

Servants. My lord? my lord?
Timon. I will dispatch you severally. You to Lord
    Lucius, to Lord Lucullus you, I hunted with his

honour to-day; you to Sempronius; commend me
to their loves; and I am proud, say, that my oc-   200
casions have found time to use 'em toward a sup-
ply of money: let the request be fifty talents.
Flaminius. As you have said, my lord.
Flavius. (*aside*) Lord Lucius and Lucullus? hum!
Timon. Go you, sir, to the senators—
  Of whom, even to the state's best health, I have
  Deserv'd this hearing—bid 'em send o' the instant
  A thousand talents to me.
Flavius.   I have been bold,
  (For that I knew it the most general way)
  To them, to use your signet and your name,   210
  But they do shake their heads, and I am here
  No richer in return.
Timon.   Is 't true? can't be?
Flavius. They answer in a joint and corporate voice,
  That now they are at fall, want treasure, cannot
  Do what they would, are sorry: you are honour-
      able,
  But yet they could have wish'd—they know not—
  Something hath been amiss; a noble nature
  May catch a wrench; would all were well; 'tis
      pity:—
  And so, intending other serious matters,
  After distasteful looks and these hard fractions,   220
  With certain half-caps and cold-moving nods
  They froze me into silence.
Timon.   You gods, reward them!
  Prithee, man, look cheerly. These old fellows
  Have their ingratitude in them hereditary:
  Their blood is cak'd, 'tis cold, it seldom flows,

'Tis lack of kindly warmth, they are not kind;
And nature, as it grows again toward earth,
Is fashion'd for the journey, dull and heavy.
(*To a Servant*) Go to Ventidius. (*to Flavius*)
    Prithee, be not sad;
Thou art true and honest; ingeniously I speak,   230
No blame belongs to thee. (*to Servant*) Ven-
    tidius lately
Buried his father, by whose death he's stepp'd
Into a great estate: when he was poor,
Imprison'd, and in scarcity of friends,
I clear'd him with five talents: greet him from
    me,
Bid him suppose some good necessity
Touches his friend, which craves to be remem-
    ber'd
With those five talents. (*exit Servant.*) (*to Fla-
    vius*) That had, giv 't these fellows
To whom 'tis instant due. Ne'er speak, or think
That Timon's fortunes 'mong his friends can sink.   240
Flavius. I would I could not think it: that thought
    is bounty's foe;
Being free itself, it thinks all others so.   *Exeunt*

Act Third

A room in Lucullus's house

Flaminius waiting. Enter a Servant to him

Servant. I have told my lord of you, he is coming
down to you.

Flaminius. I thank you, sir.

Enter Lucullus

Servant. Here's my lord.

Lucullus. (*aside*) One of Lord Timon's men? a gift,
I warrant. Why, this hits right; I dreamt of a
silver basin and ewer to-night. Flaminius, honest
Flaminius, you are very respectively welcome,
sir. Fill me some wine. (*exit Servant.*) And how
does that honourable, complete, free-hearted
gentleman of Athens, thy very bountiful good   10
lord and master?

Flaminius. His health is well, sir.

Lucullus. I am right glad that his health is well,
sir: and what hast thou there under thy cloak,
pretty Flaminius?

Flaminius. Faith, nothing but an empty box, sir,
which, in my lord's behalf, I come to entreat your
honour to supply: who, having great and instant
occasion to use fifty talents, hath sent to your

35

lordship to furnish him; nothing doubting your   20
present assistance therein.

Lucullus. La, la, la, la! 'nothing doubting,' says he?
Alas, good lord! a noble gentleman 'tis, if he
would not keep so good a house. Many a time
and often I ha' dined with him, and told him on 't,
and come again to supper to him of purpose, to
have him spend less, and yet he would embrace
no counsel, take no warning by my coming; every
man has his fault, and honesty is his. I ha' told
him on 't, but I could ne'er get him from 't.   30

Re-enter Servant, with wine

Servant. Please your lordship, here is the wine.

Lucullus. Flaminius, I have noted thee always wise.
Here's to thee.

Flaminius. Your lordship speaks your pleasure.

Lucullus. I have observed thee always for a to-
wardly prompt spirit—give thee thy due—and one
that knows what belongs to reason; and canst use
the time well, if the time use thee well. Good
parts in thee—(*to Servant*) get you gone, sirrah.
(*exit Servant.*) Draw nearer, honest Flaminius.   40
Thy lord's a bountiful gentleman, but thou art
wise, and thou know'st well enough (although
thou com'st to me) that this is no time to lend
money, especially upon bare friendship without
security. Here's three solidares for thee: good
boy, wink at me, and say thou saw'st me not.
Fare thee well.

Flaminius. Is 't possible the world should so much
differ,

And we alive that liv'd? Fly, damned baseness,   †
To him that worships thee!   50
                    Throwing back the money
Lucullus. Ha? now I see thou art a fool, and fit for
    thy master.   *Exit*
Flaminius. May these add to the number that may
    scald thee!
Let molten coin be thy damnation,
Thou disease of a friend, and not himself:
Has friendship such a faint and milky heart,
It turns in less than two nights? O you gods,
I feel my master's passion. This slave,
Unto his honour, has my lord's meat in him:
Why should it thrive, and turn to nutriment,   60
When he is turn'd to poison?
O, may diseases only work upon 't:
And, when he's sick to death, let not that part of
    nature
Which my lord paid for, be of any power
To expel sickness, but prolong his hour!   *Exit*

A public place

Enter Lucius, with three Strangers

Lucius. Who, the Lord Timon? He is my very good
    friend and an honourable gentleman.
First Stran. We know him for no less, though we
    are but strangers to him. But I can tell you one
    thing, my lord, and which I hear from common

rumours, now Lord Timon's happy hours are done
and past, and his estate shrinks from him.

Lucius. Fie, no, do not believe it: he cannot want
for money.

Sec. Stran. But believe you this, my lord, that not   10
long ago one of his men was with the Lord
Lucullus to borrow so many talents, nay, urg'd
extremely for 't, and showed what necessity
belong'd to 't, and yet was denied.

Lucius. How?

Sec. Stran. I tell you, denied, my lord.

Lucius. What a strange case was that! now, before
the gods, I am asham'd on 't. Denied that honourable man? there was very little honour show'd
in 't. For my own part, I must needs confess, I   20
have received some small kindnesses from him,
as money, plate, jewels, and suchlike trifles; nothing comparing to his: yet, had he mistook him,
and sent to me, I should ne'er have denied his
occasion so many talents.

Enter Servilius

Servilius. See, by good hap, yonder's my lord, I
have sweat to see his honour. My honour'd lord!

Lucius. Servilius? you are kindly met, sir. Fare thee
well, commend me to thy honourable virtuous
lord, my very exquisite friend.   30

Servilius. May it please your honour, my lord hath
sent—

Lucius. Ha? what has he sent? I am so much endear'd to that lord; he's ever sending: how shall

I thank him, think'st thou? And what has he sent
now?

Servilius. Has only sent his present occasion now,
my lord: requesting your lordship to supply his
instant use with so many talents.

Lucius. I know his lordship is but merry with me,   40
He cannot want fifty five hundred talents.   †

Servilius. But in the mean time he wants less, my
lord.
If his occasion were not virtuous,
I should not urge it half so faithfully.

Lucius. Dost thou speak seriously, Servilius?

Servilius. Upon my soul, 'tis true, sir.

Lucius. What a wicked beast was I to disfurnish
myself against such a good time, when I might
ha' shown myself honourable! how unluckily it
happened, that I should purchase the day before   50
for a little part, and undo a great deal of honour!
Servilius, now, before the gods, I am not able to
do—the more beast, I say:—I was sending to use
Lord Timon myself, these gentlemen can witness; but I would not for the wealth of Athens
I had done 't now. Commend me bountifully to
his good lordship, and I hope his honour will conceive the fairest of me, because I have no power
to be kind. And tell him this from me, I count it
one of my greatest afflictions, say, that I cannot   60
pleasure such an honourable gentleman. Good
Servilius, will you befriend me so far as to use
mine own words to him?

Servilius. Yes, sir, I shall.

39

Lucius. I'll look you out a good turn, Servilius.

                                    Exit Servilius

True, as you said, Timon is shrunk indeed,
And he that's once denied will hardly speed.

                                            Exit

First Stran. Do you observe this, Hostilius?
Sec. Stran.   Ay, too well.
First Stran. Why, this is the world's soul, and just
   of the same piece
Is every flatterer's spirit: who can call him   70
His friend that dips in the same dish? for, in
My knowing, Timon has been this lord's father,
And kept his credit with his purse;
Supported his estate, nay, Timon's money
Has paid his men their wages. He ne'er drinks,
But Timon's silver treads upon his lip,
And yet, O see the monstrousness of man,
When he looks out in an ungrateful shape,
He does deny him, in respect of his,
What charitable men afford to beggars.   80
Third Stran. Religion groans at it.
First Stran.   For mine own part,
I never tasted Timon in my life,
Nor came any of his bounties over me,
To mark me for his friend. Yet, I protest,
For his right noble mind, illustrious virtue,
And honourable carriage,
Had his necessity made use of me,
I would have put my wealth into donation,
And the best half should have return'd to him,
So much I love his heart: but, I perceive,   90

Men must learn now with pity to dispense,
For policy sits above conscience.   *Exeunt*

A room in Sempronius' house

Enter Sempronius, and a Servant of Timon's

Sempronius. Must he needs trouble me in 't,—hum!
    —'bove all others?
  He might have tried Lord Lucius, or Lucullus,
  And now Ventidius is wealthy too,
  Whom he redeem'd from prison. All these
  Owe their estates unto him.
Servant.   My lord,
  They have all been touch'd, and found base metal,
    for
  They all have denied him.
Sempronius.   How? have they denied him?
  Has Ventidius and Lucullus denied him,
  And does he send to me? Three? hum!
  It shows but little love, or judgement in him.   10
  Must I be his last refuge? His friends, like phy-
    sicians,
  Thrive, give him over: must I take the cure upon   †
    me?
  Has much disgrac'd me in 't, I'm angry at him,
  That might have known my place. I see no sense
    for 't,
  But his occasions might have woo'd me first;

41

For, in my conscience, I was the first man
That e'er received gift from him,
And does he think so backwardly of me now,
That I'll requite it last? No:
So it may prove an argument of laughter   20
To the rest, and 'mongst lords I be thought a fool.
I'd rather than the worth of thrice the sum,
Had sent to me first, but for my mind's sake;
I'd such a courage to do him good. But now
    return,
And with their faint reply this answer join;
Who bates mine honour shall not know my coin.
                                             Exit
Servant. Excellent! Your lordship's a goodly villain:
    the devil knew not what he did when he made
    man politic; he crossed himself by 't: and I can-
    not think but in the end the villanies of man will   30
    set him clear. How fairly this lord strives to ap-
    pear foul! takes virtuous copies to be wicked:
    like those that under hot ardent zeal would set
    whole realms on fire,
Of such a nature is his politic love.
This was my lord's best hope; now all are fled,
Save only the gods. Now his friends are dead,
Doors, that were ne'er acquainted with their
    wards
Many a bounteous year, must be employ'd
Now to guard sure their master: 40
And this is all a liberal course allows,
Who cannot keep his wealth must keep his house.
                                             Exit

SCENE IV

A hall in Timon's house

Enter two Servants of Varro, and the Servant of Lucius,
meeting Titus, Hortensius, and other Servants of Timon's
creditors, waiting his coming out

First Var. Serv. Well met; good morrow, Titus and
 Hortensius.
Titus. The like to you, kind Varro.
Hortensius.   Lucius!
 What, do we meet together?
Luc. Serv.   Ay, and I think
 One business does command us all. For mine
 Is money.
Titus. So is theirs, and ours.

Enter Philotus

Luc. Serv.   And, sir, Philotus too!
Philotus. Good day at once.
Luc. Serv.   Welcome, good brother.
 What do you think the hour?
Philotus.   Labouring for nine.
Luc. Serv. So much?
Philotus.   Is not my lord seen yet?
Luc. Serv.   Not yet.
Philotus. I wonder on 't, he was wont to shine at
 seven.   10
Luc. Serv. Ay, but the days are wax'd shorter with
 him:
 You must consider that a prodigal course

43

Is like the sun's, but not like his recoverable,
I fear
'Tis deepest winter in Lord Timon's purse,
That is, one may reach deep enough, and yet
Find little.

Philotus.　I am of your fear for that.

Titus. I'll show you how to observe a strange event:
Your lord sends now for money?

Hortensius.　　　　Most true, he does.

Titus. And he wears jewels now of Timon's gift,　　20
For which I wait for money.

Hortensius. It is against my heart.

Luc. Serv.　　　Mark, how strange it shows,
Timon, in this, should pay more than he owes:
And e'en as if your lord should wear rich jewels,
And send for money for 'em.

Hortensius. I'm weary of this charge, the gods can
witness:
I know my lord hath spent of Timon's wealth,
And now ingratitude makes it worse than stealth.

First Var. Serv. Yes, mine's three thousand crowns:
what's yours?

Luc. Serv. Five thousand mine.　　　　30

First Var. Serv. 'Tis much deep, and it should seem
by the sum
Your master's confidence was above mine,
Else surely his had equall'd.

Enter Flaminius

Titus. One of Lord Timon's men.

Luc. Serv. Flaminius! Sir, a word: pray, is my lord
ready to come forth?

Flaminius. No, indeed he is not.

Titus. We attend his lordship: pray, signify so much.

Flaminius. I need not tell him that, he knows you
  are too diligent.   *Exit*   40

Enter Flavius in a cloak, muffled

Luc. Serv. Ha! is not that his steward muffled so?
  He goes away in a cloud: call him, call him.

Titus. Do you hear, sir?

Sec. Var. Serv. By your leave, sir,—

Flavius. What do ye ask of me, my friend?

Titus. We wait for certain money here, sir.

Flavius.   Ay,
  If money were as certain as your waiting,
  'Twere sure enough.
  Why then preferr'd you not your sums and bills,
  When your false masters ate of my lord's meat?   50
  Then they could smile, and fawn upon his debts,
  And take down the interest into their gluttonous
      maws.
  You do yourselves but wrong, to stir me up,
  Let me pass quietly:
  Believe 't, my lord and I have made an end,
  I have no more to reckon, he to spend.

Luc. Serv. Ay, but this answer will not serve.

Flavius. If 'twill not serve, 'tis not so base as you,
  For you serve knaves.   *Exit*

First Var. Serv. How? what does his cashier'd wor-   60
  ship mutter?

Sec. Var. Serv. No matter what, he's poor, and that's
  revenge enough. Who can speak broader than he

45

that has no house to put his head in? Such may
rail against great buildings.

Enter Servilius

Titus. O, here's Servilius: now we shall know some
answer.

Servilius. If I might beseech you, gentlemen, to
repair some other hour, I should derive much
from 't. For, take 't of my soul, my lord leans   70
wondrously to discontent: his comfortable temper has forsook him, he's much out of health,
and keeps his chamber.

Luc. Serv. Many do keep their chambers are not
sick:
And if it be so far beyond his health,
Methinks he should the sooner pay his debts,
And make a clear way to the gods.

Servilius.   Good gods!

Titus. We cannot take this for answer, sir.

Flaminius. (*within*) Servilius, help! My lord! my
lord!

Enter Timon, in a rage; Flaminius following

Timon. What, are my doors oppos'd against my
passage?   80
Have I been ever free, and must my house
Be my retentive enemy? my gaol?
The place which I have feasted, does it now,
(Like all mankind) show me an iron heart?

Luc. Serv. Put in now, Titus.

Titus. My lord, here is my bill.

Luc. Serv. Here's mine.

Hortensius. And mine, my lord.
Both Var. Serv. And ours, my lord.
Philotus. All our bills. 90
Timon. Knock me down with 'em, cleave me to the
    girdle.
Luc. Serv. Alas, my lord,—
Timon. Cut my heart in sums.
Titus. Mine, fifty talents.
Timon. Tell out my blood.
Luc. Serv. Five thousand crowns, my lord.
Timon. Five thousand drops pays that. What yours?
    —and yours?
First Var. Serv. My lord,—
Sec. Var. Serv. My lord,— 100
Timon. Tear me, take me, and the gods fall upon
    you! *Exit*
Hortensius. Faith, I perceive our masters may throw
   their caps at their money, these debts may well be
   called desperate ones, for a madman owes 'em.
                           Exeunt

Re-enter Timon and Flavius

Timon. They have e'en put my breath from me, the
    slaves.
    Creditors? devils!
Flavius. My dear lord,—
Timon. What if it should be so?
Flavius. My lord,—
Timon. I'll have it so. My steward! 110
Flavius. Here, my lord.
Timon. So fitly? Go, bid all my friends again,
    Lucius, Lucullus, and Sempronius: all: †

I'll once more feast the rascals.

Flavius.   O my lord,
You only speak from your distracted soul;
There's not so much left, to furnish out
A moderate table.

Timon.   Be it not in thy care; go,
I charge thee, invite them all, let in the tide
Of knaves once more; my cook and I'll provide.

                                        Exeunt

SCENE V

The Senate-house

Enter three Senators

First Sen. My lord, you have my voice; to 't: the
    fault's
Bloody; 'tis necessary he should die:
Nothing emboldens sin so much as mercy.
Sec. Sen. Most true; the law shall bruise 'em.

Enter Alcibiades, attended

Alcibiades. Honour, health, and compassion to the
    senate!
First Sen. Now, captain?
Alcibiades. I am an humble suitor to your virtues;
For pity is the virtue of the law,
And none but tyrants use it cruelly.
It pleases time and fortune to lie heavy   10
Upon a friend of mine, who in hot blood
Hath stepp'd into the law; which is past depth
To those that (without heed) do plunge into 't.

48

He is a man, (setting his fate aside)
Of comely virtues,
Nor did he soil the fact with cowardice
(An honour in him which buys out his fault)
But with a noble fury, and fair spirit,
Seeing his reputation touch'd to death,
He did oppose his foe: 20
And with such sober and unnoted passion
He did behoove his anger, ere 'twas spent,   †
As if he had but prov'd an argument.
First Sen. You undergo too strict a paradox,
  Striving to make an ugly deed look fair:
  Your words have took such pains, as if they la-
    bour'd
  To bring manslaughter into form, and set quar-
    relling
  Upon the head of valour; which indeed
  Is valour misbegot, and came into the world
  When sects and factions were newly born.   30
  He's truly valiant, that can wisely suffer
  The worst that man can breathe, and make his
    wrongs
  His outsides, to wear them like his raiment, care-
    lessly
  And ne'er prefer his injuries to his heart,
  To bring it into danger.
  If wrongs be evils and enforce us kill,
  What folly 'tis to hazard life for ill!
Alcibiades. My lord,—
First Sen. You cannot make gross sins look clear:
  To revenge is no valour, but to bear.

49

Alcibiades. My lords, then, under favour, pardon
    me,   40
  If I speak like a captain.
  Why do fond men expose themselves to battle,
  And not endure all threats? sleep upon 't,
  And let the foes quietly cut their throats,
  Without repugnancy? If there be
  Such valour in the bearing, what make we
  Abroad? Why then, women are more valiant
  That stay at home, if bearing carry it:
  And the ass more captain than the lion? the
    fellow
  Loaden with irons wiser then the judge?   50
  If wisdom be in suffering. O my lords,
  As you are great, be pitifully good:
  Who cannot condemn rashness in cold blood?
  To kill, I grant, is sin's extremest gust,
  But in defence, by mercy, 'tis most just.
  To be in anger is impiety;
  But who is man that is not angry?
  Weigh but the crime with this.
Sec. Sen. You breathe in vain.
Alcibiades.   In vain? His service done
  At Lacedæmon, and Byzantium,   60
  Were a sufficient briber for his life.
First Sen. What's that?
Alcibiades.   I say, my lords, has done fair service,
  And slain in fight many of your enemies:
  How full of valour did he bear himself
  In the last conflict, and made plenteous wounds!

Sec. Sen. He has made too much plenty with 'em;
He's a sworn rioter, he has a sin
That often drowns him, and takes his valour
  prisoner.
If there were no foes, that were enough
To overcome him. In that beastly fury   70
He has been known to commit outrages,
And cherish factions. 'Tis inferr'd to us,
His days are foul, and his drink dangerous.
First Sen. He dies.
Alcibiades.   Hard fate! he might have died in war.
My lords, if not for any parts in him,
Though his right arm might purchase his own
  time,
And be in debt to none, yet, more to move you,
Take my deserts to his, and join 'em both:
And, for I know your reverend ages love
Security, I'll pawn my victories, all   80
My honour to you, upon his good returns.
If by this crime he owes the law his life,
Why, let the war receive 't in valiant gore,
For law is strict, and war is nothing more.
First Sen. We are for law, he dies, urge it no more,
On height of our displeasure: friend, or brother,
He forfeits his own blood that spills another.
Alcibiades. Must it be so? it must not be: my lords,
I do beseech you, know me.
Sec. Sen. How?   90
Alcibiades. Call me to your remembrances.
Third Sen. What?

51

Alcibiades. I cannot think but your age has forgot
    me,
  It could not else be I should prove so base,
  To sue and be denied such common grace:
  My wounds ache at you.
First Sen.   Do you dare our anger?
  'Tis in few words, but spacious in effect:
  We banish thee for ever.
Alcibiades.   Banish me?
  Banish your dotage, banish usury,
  That makes the senate ugly.   100
First Sen. If, after two days' shine, Athens contain
    thee,
  Attend our weightier judgement. And, not to
    swell our spirit,
  He shall be executed presently.   *Exeunt Senators*
Alcibiades. Now the gods keep you old enough, that
    you may live
  Only in bone, that none may look on you!
  I'm worse than mad: I have kept back their foes,
  While they have told their money, and let out
  Their coin upon large interest; I myself
  Rich only in large hurts. All those, for this?
  Is this the balsam, that the usuring senate   110
  Pours into captains' wounds? Banishment!
  It comes not ill: I hate not to be banish'd,
  It is a cause worthy my spleen and fury,
  That I may strike at Athens. I'll cheer up
  My discontented troops, and lay for hearts;
  'Tis honour with most lands to be at odds,
  Soldiers should brook as little wrongs as gods.
                                          Exit

SCENE VI

A banqueting-room in Timon's house

*Music. Tables set out: Servants attending. Enter divers
Lords, Senators and others, at several doors*

First Lord. The good time of day to you, sir.

Sec. Lord. I also wish it to you: I think this honourable lord did but try us this other day.

First Lord. Upon that were my thoughts tiring when
we encounter'd: I hope it is not so low with him
as he made it seem in the trial of his several
friends.

Sec. Lord. It should not be, by the persuasion of his
new feasting.

First Lord. I should think so. He hath sent me an   10
earnest inviting, which many my near occasions
did urge me to put off: but he hath conjur'd me
beyond them, and I must needs appear.

Sec. Lord. In like manner was I in debt to my importunate business, but he would not hear my
excuse. I am sorry, when he sent to borrow of
me, that my provision was out.

First Lord. I am sick of that grief too, as I understand how all things go.

Sec. Lord. Every man here's so: what would he   20
have borrowed of you?

First Lord. A thousand pieces.

Sec. Lord. A thousand pieces?

First Lord. What of you?

Sec. Lord. He sent to me, sir,—Here he comes.

53

Enter Timon and Attendants

Timon. With all my heart, gentlemen both; and how fare you?

First Lord. Ever at the best, hearing well of your lordship.

Sec. Lord. The swallow follows not summer more 30 willing than we your lordship.

Timon. (*aside*) Nor more willingly leaves winter, such summer-birds are men.—Gentlemen, our dinner will not recompense this long stay: feast your ears with the music awhile, if they will fare so harshly o' the trumpet's sound; we shall to 't presently.

First Lord. I hope it remains not unkindly with your lordship, that I return'd you an empty messenger. 40

Timon. O, sir, let it not trouble you.

Sec. Lord. My noble lord,—

Timon. Ay, my good friend, what cheer?

Sec. Lord. My most honourable lord, I am e'en sick of shame, that, when your lordship this other day sent to me, I was so unfortunate a beggar.

Timon. Think not on 't, sir.

Sec. Lord. If you had sent but two hours before—

Timon. Let it not cumber your better remembrance. (*The banquet brought in.*) Come, bring in all 50 together.

Sec. Lord. All cover'd dishes!

First Lord. Royal cheer, I warrant you.

Third Lord. Doubt not that, if money and the season can yield it.

First Lord. How do you? What's the news?

Third Lord. Alcibiades is banish'd: heard you of it?

First and Sec. Lords. Alcibiades banish'd?

Third Lord. 'Tis so, be sure of it.

First Lord. How? how?   60

Sec. Lord. I pray you, upon what?

Timon. My worthy friends, will you draw near?

Third Lord. I'll tell you more anon. Here's a noble
  feast toward.

Sec. Lord. This is the old man still.

Third Lord. Will 't hold? will 't hold?

Sec. Lord. It does: but time will—and so—

Third Lord. I do conceive.

Timon. Each man to his stool, with that spur as he
  would to the lip of his mistress: your diet shall be   70
  in all places alike. Make not a city feast of it, to
  let the meat cool, ere we can agree upon the first
  place. Sit, sit. The gods require our thanks.

      You great benefactors, sprinkle our society
  with thankfulness. For your own gifts, make yourselves prais'd: but reserve still to give, lest your
  deities be despis'd. Lend to each man enough,
  that one need not lend to another. For, were your
  godheads to borrow of men, men would for-
  sake the gods. Make the meat be belov'd, more   80
  than the man that gives it. Let no assembly of
  twenty be without a score of villains. If there sit
  twelve women at the table, let a dozen of them be
  as they are. The rest of your fees, O gods,—the
  senators of Athens, together with the common
  lag of people,—what is amiss in them, you gods,

55

make suitable for destruction. For these my
present friends, as they are to me nothing, so in
nothing bless them, and to nothing are they wel-
come.   90

Uncover, dogs, and lap.

Some speak. What does his lordship mean?

Some other. I know not.

> *The dishes are uncovered and seen to be*
> *full of warm water*

Timon. May you a better feast never behold,
You knot of mouth-friends! smoke and luke-warm
    water
Is your perfection. This is Timon's last
Who stuck and spangled you with flatteries,
Washes it off, and sprinkles in your faces
Your reeking villainy.

> (*Throwing the water in their faces*)
>   Live loath'd, and long,

Most smiling, smooth, detested parasites,   100
Courteous destroyers, affable wolves, meek bears:
You fools of fortune, trencher-friends, time's flies,
Cap-and-knee slaves, vapours, and minute-jacks!
Of man and beast the infinite malady
Crust you quite o'er! What, dost thou go?
Soft, take thy physic first; thou too, and thou:
Stay, I will lend thee money, borrow none.
What? all in motion? Henceforth be no feast,
Whereat a villain's not a welcome guest.
Burn, house! sink, Athens! henceforth hated be   110
Of Timon man and all humanity!   *Exit*

Re-enter the Lords, Senators, &c.

First Lord. How now, my lords!

Sec. Lord. Know you the quality of Lord Timon's
fury?

Third Lord. Push! did you see my cap?

Fourth Lord. I have lost my gown.

First Lord. He's but a mad lord, and nought but hu-
mours sways him. He gave me a jewel th' other
day, and now he has beat it out of my hat. Did
you see my jewel?   120

Third Lord. Did you see my cap?

Sec. Lord. Here 'tis.

Fourth Lord. Here lies my gown.

First Lord. Let's make no stay.

Sec. Lord. Lord Timon's mad.

Third Lord.   I feel 't upon my bones.

Fourth Lord. One day he gives us diamonds, next
day stones.   *Exeunt*

Act Fourth

SCENE I

Without the walls of Athens

Enter Timon

Timon. Let me look back upon thee. O thou wall,
That girdles in those wolves, dive in the earth,
And fence not Athens! Matrons, turn incontinent,
Obedience fail in children: slaves and fools

57

Pluck the grave wrinkled senate from the bench,
And minister in their steads; to general filths
Convert o' the instant green virginity,
Do 't in your parents' eyes! Bankrupts, hold fast,
Rather than render back; out with your knives,
And cut your trusters' throats! Bound servants,
    steal!   10
Large-handed robbers your grave masters are,
And pill by law. Maid, to thy master's bed,
Thy mistress is o' the brothel. Son of sixteen,
Pluck the lin'd crutch from thy old limping sire,
With it beat out his brains! Piety, and fear,
Religion to the gods, peace, justice, truth,
Domestic awe, night-rest, and neighbourhood,
Instruction, manners, mysteries, and trades,
Degrees, observances, customs, and laws,
Decline to your confounding contraries.   20
And yet confusion live: plagues incident to men,
Your potent and infectious fevers, heap
On Athens, ripe for stroke! Thou cold sciatica,
Cripple our senators, that their limbs may halt
As lamely as their manners! Lust, and liberty
That 'gainst the stream of virtue they may strive,
Creep in the minds and marrows of our youth,
And drown themselves in riot! Itches, blains,
Sow all the Athenian bosoms, and their crop
Be general leprosy: breath, infect breath,   30
That their society (as their friendship) may
Be merely poison! Nothing I'll bear from thee
But nakedness, thou detestable town,
Take thou that too, with multiplying bans!
Timon will to the woods, where he shall find

The unkindest beast more kinder than mankind.
The gods confound—hear me, you good gods all!—
The Athenians both within and out that wall!
And grant, as Timon grows, his hate may grow
To the whole race of mankind, high and low!   40
Amen.   *Exit*

SCENE II

Athens. Timon's house

Enter Flavius, with two or three Servants

First Serv. Hear you, master steward, where's our
      master?
   Are we undone? cast off? nothing remaining?
Flavius. Alack, my fellows, what should I say to
      you?
   Let me be recorded by the righteous gods,
   I am as poor as you.
First Serv.   Such a house broke?
   So noble a master fall'n, all gone, and not
   One friend to take his fortune by the arm,
   And go along with him?
Sec. Serv.   As we do turn our backs
   From our companion, thrown into his grave,
   So his familiars to his buried fortunes   10
   Slink all away, leave their false vows with him
   Like empty purses pick'd; and his poor self,
   A dedicated beggar to the air,
   With his disease of all-shunn'd poverty,
   Walks, like contempt, alone. More of our fellows.

Enter other Servants

59

Flavius. All broken implements of a ruin'd house.
Third Serv. Yet do our hearts wear Timon's livery,
 That see I by our faces: we are fellows still,
 Serving alike in sorrow: leak'd is our bark,
 And we, poor mates, stand on the dying deck,   20
 Hearing the surges threat: we must all part
 Into this sea of air.
Flavius.   Good fellows all,
 The latest of my wealth I'll share amongst you.
 Wherever we shall meet, for Timon's sake
 Let's yet be fellows. Let's shake our heads, and
  say,
 As 'twere a knell unto our master's fortunes,
 'We have seen better days.' Let each take some:
 Nay, put out all your hands: not one word more,
 Thus part we rich in sorrow, parting poor.
     Servants embrace, and part several ways
O, the fierce wretchedness that glory brings us!   30
Who would not wish to be from wealth exempt,
Since riches point to misery and contempt?
Who would be so mock'd with glory? or to live
But in a dream of friendship,
To have his pomp, and all what state compounds,
But only painted like his varnish'd friends?
Poor honest lord, brought low by his own heart,
Undone by goodness! Strange, unusual blood,
When man's worst sin is, he does too much good!
Who then dares to be half so kind again?   40
For bounty, that makes gods, does still mar men.
My dearest lord, blest to be most accurs'd,
Rich only to be wretched; thy great fortunes
Are made thy chief afflictions. Alas (kind lord)

He's flung in rage from this ingrateful seat
Of monstrous friends: nor has he with him to
Supply his life, or that which can command it:
I'll follow and inquire him out.
I'll ever serve his mind, with my best will;
Whilst I have gold, I'll be his steward still.   *Exit*   50

SCENE III

and

Act Fifth: SCENE I

The woods

Enter Timon

Timon. O blessed breeding sun, draw from the earth
Rotten humidity: below thy sister's orb
Infect the air! Twinn'd brothers of one womb,
Whose procreation, residence, and birth
Scarce is dividant, touch them with several for-
tunes
The greater scorns the lesser. Not nature,
(To whom all sores lay siege) can bear great
fortune
But by contempt of nature.
Raise me this beggar, and deny 't that lord,
The senator shall bear contempt hereditary,   10
The beggar native honour.
It is the pasture lards the rother's sides,
The want that makes him lean. Who dares, who
dares,
In purity of manhood stand upright,

61

And say 'This man's a flatterer'? if one be,
So are they all: for every grise of fortune
Is smooth'd by that below. The learned pate
Ducks to the golden fool. All's obliquy;
There's nothing level in our cursed natures
But direct villainy. Therefore be abhorr'd,   20
All feasts, societies, and throngs of men!
His semblable, yea, himself, Timon disdains:
Destruction fang mankind! Earth yield me roots,
                                        Digging
Who seeks for better of thee, sauce his palate
With thy most operant poison! What is here?
Gold? Yellow, glittering, precious gold? No, gods,
I am no idle votarist: roots, you clear heavens!
Thus much of this will make black, white; foul,
     fair;
Wrong, right; base, noble; old, young; coward,
     valiant.
Ha, you gods! why this? what this, you gods?
     Why, this   30
Will lug your priests and servants from your
     sides;
Pluck stout men's pillows from below their heads:
This yellow slave
Will knit and break religions, bless the accurs'd,
Make the hoar leprosy ador'd, place thieves,
And give them title, knee, and approbation
With senators on the bench: this is it
That makes the wapper'd widow wed again;
She, whom the spital-house, and ulcerous sores
Would cast the gorge at, this embalms and spices   40
To the April day again. Come, damn'd earth,

Thou common whore of mankind, that puts odds
Among the rout of nations, I will make thee
Do thy right nature. (*March afar off.*) Ha? a
    drum? Thou'rt quick,
But yet I'll bury thee: thou'lt go (strong thief)
When gouty keepers of thee cannot stand:
Nay, stay thou out for earnest.

                            Keeping some gold

Enter Alcibiades, with drum and fife, in warlike manner;
Phrynia and Timandra

Alcibiades.   What art thou there? speak.
Timon. A beast as thou art. The canker gnaw thy
    heart,
For showing me again the eyes of man!
Alcibiades. What is thy name? Is man so hateful
    to thee,   50
That art thyself a man?
Timon. I am misanthropos, and hate mankind.
For thy part, I do wish thou wert a dog,
That I might love thee something.
Alcibiades.   I know thee well:
But in thy fortunes am unlearn'd and strange.
Timon. I know thee too, and more than that I know
    thee
I not desire to know. Follow thy drum!
With man's blood paint the ground gules, gules:
Religious canons, civil laws are cruel,
Then what should war be? This fell whore of
    thine   60
Hath in her more destruction than thy sword,
For all her cherubin look.

Phrynia.   Thy lips rot off!

Timon. I will not kiss thee, then the rot returns
   To thine own lips again.

Alcibiades. How came the noble Timon to this
   change?

Timon. As the moon does, by wanting light to give:
   But then renew I could not like the moon,
   There were no suns to borrow of.

Alcibiades.   Noble Timon,
   What friendship may I do thee?

Timon.   None, but to
   Maintain my opinion.   70

Alcibiades. What is it, Timon?

Timon. Promise me friendship, but perform none.
   If thou wilt not promise, the gods plague thee,
   for thou art a man: if thou dost perform, confound thee, for thou art a man!

Alcibiades. I have heard in some sort of thy miseries.

Timon. Thou saw'st them when I had prosperity.

Alcibiades. I see them now; then was a blessed time.

Timon. As thine is now, held with a brace of harlots.

Timandra. Is this the Athenian minion, whom the
   world   80
   Voic'd so regardfully?

Timon.   Art thou Timandra?

Timandra. Yes.

Timon. Be a whore still: they love thee not that use
   thee;
   Give them diseases, leaving with thee their lust.
   Make use of thy salt hours, season the slaves
   For tubs and baths, bring down rose-cheeked
   youth

To the tub-fast, and the diet.
Timandra.   Hang thee, monster!
Alcibiades. Pardon him, sweet Timandra, for his
    wits
    Are drown'd and lost in his calamities.
    I have but little gold of late, brave Timon,   90
    The want whereof doth daily make revolt
    In my penurious band: I have heard, and griev'd,
    How cursed Athens, mindless of thy worth,
    Forgetting thy great deeds, when neighbour
    states,
    But for thy sword and fortune, trod upon them—
Timon. I prithee, beat thy drum, and get thee gone.
Alcibiades. I am thy friend, and pity thee, dear
    Timon.
Timon. How dost thou pity him whom thou dost
    trouble?
    I had rather be alone.
Alcibiades.   Why, fare thee well:
    Here is some gold for thee.
Timon.   Keep it, I cannot eat it.   100
Alcibiades. When I have laid proud Athens on a
    heap—
Timon. Warr'st thou 'gainst Athens?
Alcibiades.   Ay, Timon, and have cause.
Timon. The gods confound them all in thy conquest,
    And thee after, when thou hast conquered!
Alcibiades. Why me, Timon?
Timon.   That by killing of villains
    Thou wast born to conquer my country.
    Put up thy gold. Go on, here's gold, go on;
    Be as a planetary plague, when Jove

Will o'er some high-vic'd city hang his poison
In the sick air: let not thy sword skip one: 110
Pity not honour'd age for his white beard,
He is an usurer. Strike me the counterfeit matron,
It is her habit only, that is honest,
Herself's a bawd. Let not the virgin's cheek
Make soft thy trenchant sword; for those milk-
        paps,
That through the window-bars bore at men's eyes,
Are not within the leaf of pity writ,
But set them down horrible traitors. Spare not the
        babe
Whose dimpled smiles from fools exhaust their
        mercy;
Think it a bastard, whom the oracle   120
Hath doubtfully pronounc'd the throat shall cut,
And mince it sans remorse. Swear against objects,
Put armour on thine ears; and on thine eyes,
Whose proof nor yells of mothers, maids, nor
        babes,
Nor sight of priests in holy vestments bleeding,
Shall pierce a jot. There's gold to pay thy soldiers,
Make large confusion: and, thy fury spent,
Confounded be thyself! Speak not, be gone.
Alcibiades. Hast thou gold yet? I'll take the gold
        thou giv'st me,
Not all thy counsel.   130
Timon. Dost thou or dost thou not, heaven's curse
        upon thee!
Phrynia and Timandra. Give us some gold, good
        Timon: hast thou more?

Timon. Enough to make a whore forswear her trade,
  And to make whores, a bawd. Hold up, you sluts,
  Your aprons mountant; you are not oathable,
  Although I know you'll swear, terribly swear
  Into strong shudders and to heavenly agues
  The immortal gods that hear you. Spare your
    oaths:
  I'll trust to your conditions, be whores still.
  And he whose pious breath seeks to convert you,   140
  Be strong in whore, allure him, burn him up,
  Let your close fire predominate his smoke,
  And be no turncoats: yet may your pains, six
    months,
  Be quite contrary: and thatch your poor thin
    roofs
  With burdens of the dead, (some that were
    hang'd)
  No matter:—wear them, betray with them; whore
    still,
  Paint till a horse may mire upon your face:
  A pox of wrinkles!
Phrynia and Timandra. Well, more gold, what then?
  Believe 't that we'll do any thing for gold.   150
Timon. Consumptions sow
  In hollow bones of man, strike their sharp shins,
  And mar men's spurring. Crack the lawyer's voice,
  That he may never more false title plead,
  Nor sound his quillets shrilly: hoar the flamen,
  That scolds against the quality of flesh,
  And not believes himself. Down with the nose,
  Down with it flat, take the bridge quite away
  Of him that, his particular to foresee,

Smells from the general weal. Make curl'd-pate
    ruffians bald,   160
And let the unscarr'd braggarts of the war
Derive some pain from you. Plague all,
That your activity may defeat and quell
The source of all erection. There's more gold.
Do you damn others, and let this damn you,
And ditches grave you all!
Phrynia and Timandra. More counsel with more
    money, bounteous Timon.
Timon. More whore, more mischief first; I have
    given you earnest.
Alcibiades. Strike up the drum towards Athens; fare-
    well, Timon:
If I thrive well, I'll visit thee again.   170
Timon. If I hope well, I'll never see thee more.
Alcibiades. I never did thee harm.
Timon. Yes, thou spok'st well of me.
Alcibiades.   Call'st thou that harm?
Timon. Men daily find it. Get thee away, and take
    Thy beagles with thee.
Alcibiades.   We but offend him; strike!
                   Drums beat. Exeunt Alcibiades,
                     Phrynia, and Timandra
Timon. That nature, being sick of man's unkindness,
Should yet be hungry! Common mother, thou
                               Digging
Whose womb unmeasurable, and infinite breast
Teems and feeds all: whose self-same mettle,
Whereof thy proud child, arrogant man, is puff'd,   180
Engenders the black toad, and adder blue,
The gilded newt, and eyeless venom'd worm,

With all the abhorred births below crisp heaven,
Whereon Hyperion's quickening fire doth shine:
Yield him, who all the human sons do hate,   †
From forth thy plenteous bosom, one poor root:
Ensear thy fertile and conceptious womb,
Let it no more bring out ingrateful man!
Go great with tigers, dragons, wolves, and bears;
Teem with new monsters, whom thy upward face   190
Hath to the marbled mansion all above
Never presented!—O, a root! dear thanks!—
Dry up thy marrows, vines, and plough-torn leas,
Whereof ingrateful man with liquorish draughts
And morsels unctuous greases his pure mind,
That from it all consideration slips!

Enter Apemantus

More man? plague, plague!
Apemantus. I was directed hither. Men report
Thou dost affect my manners, and dost use them.
Timon. 'Tis then because thou dost not keep a dog,   200
Whom I would imitate. Consumption catch thee!
Apemantus. This is in thee a nature but infected,
A poor unmanly melancholy sprung
From change of fortune. Why this spade? this
place?
This slave-like habit, and these looks of care?
Thy flatterers yet wear silk, drink wine, lie soft,
Hug their diseas'd perfumes, and have forgot
That ever Timon was. Shame not these woods
By putting on the cunning of a carper.
Be thou a flatterer now, and seek to thrive   210
By that which has undone thee; hinge thy knee,

And let his very breath whom thou'lt observe
Blow off thy cap: praise his most vicious strain,
And call it excellent: thou wast told thus:
Thou gav'st thine ears (like tapsters that bade
    welcome)
To knaves, and all approachers: 'tis most just
That thou turn rascal, hadst thou wealth again,
Rascals should have 't. Do not assume my likeness.
Timon. Were I like thee, I'ld throw away myself.
Apemantus. Thou hast cast away thyself, being like
    thyself,   220
A madman so long, now a fool: what, think'st
That the bleak air, thy boisterous chamberlain,
Will put thy shirt on warm? will these moss'd
    trees,
That have outliv'd the eagle, page thy heels,
And skip when thou point'st out? Will the cold
    brook,
Candied with ice, caudle thy morning taste
To cure thy o'er-night's surfeit? Call the creatures,
Whose naked natures live in all the spite
Of wreakful heaven, whose bare unhoused trunks,
To the conflicting elements expos'd,   230
Answer mere nature: bid them flatter thee.
O, thou shalt find—
Timon.   A fool of thee: depart.
Apemantus. I love thee better now than ere I did.
Timon. I hate thee worse.
Apemantus.   Why?
Timon.   Thou flatter'st misery.
Apemantus. I flatter not, but say thou art a caitiff.
Timon. Why dost thou seek me out?

Apemantus.   To vex thee.

Timon. Always a villain's office, or a fool's.

  Dost please thyself in 't?

Apemantus.   Ay.

Timon.   What, a knave too?

Apemantus. If thou didst put this sour cold habit on

  To castigate thy pride, 'twere well: but thou   240

  Dost it enforcedly: thou 'ldst courtier be again,

  Wert thou not beggar: willing misery

  Outlives incertain pomp, is crown'd before:

  The one is filling still, never complete;

  The other, at high wish: best state, contentless,

  Hath a distracted and most wretched being,

  Worse than the worst, content.

  Thou shouldst desire to die, being miserable.

Timon. Not by his breath that is more miserable.

  Thou art a slave, whom Fortune's tender arm   250

  With favour never clasp'd; but bred a dog.

  Hadst thou like us from our first swath pro-
    ceeded,

  The sweet degrees that this brief world affords

  To such as may the passive drugs of it

  Freely command, thou wouldst have plung'd thy-
    self

  In general riot, melted down thy youth

  In different beds of lust, and never learn'd

  The icy precepts of respect, but follow'd

  The sugar'd game before thee. But myself,

  Who had the world as my confectionary,   260

  The mouths, the tongues, the eyes, and hearts of
    men,

  At duty more than I could frame employment;

71

That numberless upon me stuck, as leaves
Do on the oak, have with one winter's brush
Fell from their boughs, and left me open, bare,
For every storm that blows. I to bear this,
That never knew but better, is some burden:
Thy nature did commence in sufferance, time
Hath made thee hard in 't. Why shouldst thou
 hate men?
They never flatter'd thee. What hast thou given?   270
If thou wilt curse, thy father (that poor rag)
Must be thy subject, who in spite put stuff
To some she-beggar, and compounded thee
Poor rogue, hereditary. Hence, be gone!
If thou hadst not been born the worst of men,
Thou hadst been a knave and flatterer.
Apemantus.   Art thou proud yet?
Timon. Ay, that I am not thee.
Apemantus.   I, that I was
 No prodigal.
Timon.   I, that I am one now.
Were all the wealth I have shut up in thee,
I'ld give thee leave to hang it. Get thee gone.   280
That the whole life of Athens were in this!
Thus would I eat it.   *Eating a root*
Apemantus.   Here, I will mend thy feast.
          Offering him a root
Timon. First mend my company, take away thyself.
Apemantus. So I shall mend mine own, by the lack
 of thine.
Timon. 'Tis not well mended so, it is but botch'd;
 If not, I would it were.
Apemantus. What wouldst thou have to Athens?

Timon. Thee thither in a whirlwind: if thou wilt,
Tell them there I have gold, look, so I have.
Apemantus. Here is no use for gold.
Timon.   The best, and truest: 290
For here it sleeps, and does no hired harm.
Apemantus. Where liest o' nights, Timon?
Timon.   Under that's above me.
Where feed'st thou o' days, Apemantus?
Apemantus. Where my stomach finds meat, or,
rather where I eat it.
Timon. Would poison were obedient, and knew my
mind!
Apemantus. Where wouldst thou send it?
Timon. To sauce thy dishes.
Apemantus. The middle of humanity thou never 300
knewest, but the extremity of both ends. When
thou wast in thy gilt, and thy perfume, they
mock'd thee for too much curiosity; in thy rags
thou know'st none, but art despis'd for the con-
trary. There's a medlar for thee; eat it.
Timon. On what I hate I feed not.
Apemantus. Dost hate a medlar?
Timon. Ay, though it look like thee.
Apemantus. An thou hadst hated meddlers sooner,
thou shouldst have lov'd thyself better now. What 310
man didst thou ever know unthrift that was belov'd after his means?
Timon. Who, without those means thou talk'st of,
didst thou ever know belov'd?
Apemantus. Myself.
Timon. I understand thee: thou hadst some means
to keep a dog.

Apemantus. What things in the world canst thou nearest compare to thy flatterers?

Timon. Women nearest, but men—men are the 320 things themselves. What wouldst thou do with the world, Apemantus, if it lay in thy power?

Apemantus. Give it the beasts, to be rid of the men.

Timon. Wouldst thou have thyself fall in the confusion of men, and remain a beast with the beasts?

Apemantus. Ay, Timon.

Timon. A beastly ambition, which the gods grant thee t' attain to! If thou wert the lion, the fox would beguile thee: if thou wert the lamb, the fox would eat thee: if thou wert the fox, the lion 330 would suspect thee, when peradventure thou wert accus'd by the ass: if thou wert the ass, thy dulness would torment thee; and still thou livedst but as a breakfast to the wolf. If thou wert the wolf, thy greediness would afflict thee, and oft thou shouldst hazard thy life for thy dinner. Wert thou the unicorn, pride and wrath would confound thee, and make thine own self the conquest of thy fury. Wert thou a bear, thou wouldst be kill'd by the horse: wert thou a horse, thou 340 wouldst be seiz'd by the leopard: wert thou a leopard, thou wert german to the lion, and the spots of thy kindred were jurors on thy life. All thy safety were remotion, and thy defence absence. What beast couldst thou be that were not subject to a beast? and what a beast art thou already, that seest not thy loss in transformation!

Apemantus. If thou couldst please me with speaking to me, thou mightst have hit upon it here: the

commonwealth of Athens is become a forest of 350
beasts.

Timon. How has the ass broke the wall, that thou
art out of the city?

Apemantus. Yonder comes a poet and a painter:
the plague of company light upon thee! I will fear
to catch it, and give way. When I know not what
else to do, I'll see thee again.

Timon. When there is nothing living but thee, thou
shalt be welcome. I had rather be a beggar's dog
than Apemantus. 360

Apemantus. Thou art the cap of all the fools alive.

Timon. Would thou wert clean enough to spit upon!

Apemantus. A plague on thee, thou art too bad to
curse.

Timon. All villains that do stand by thee are pure.

Apemantus. There is no leprosy but what thou
speak'st.

Timon. If I name thee,
I'll beat thee; but I should infect my hands.

Apemantus. I would my tongue could rot them off!

Timon. Away, thou issue of a mangy dog,
Choler does kill me, that thou art alive, 370
I swoon to see thee.

Apemantus. Would thou wouldst burst!

Timon. Away, thou tedious rogue, I am sorry I shall
lose a stone by thee. *Throws a stone at him*

Apemantus. Beast!

Timon. Slave!

Apemantus. Toad!

Timon. Rogue, rogue, rogue!
I am sick of this false world, and will love nought

But even the mere necessities upon 't: 380
Then, Timon, presently prepare thy grave:
Lie where the light foam of the sea may beat
Thy grave-stone daily, make thine epitaph,
That death in me at others' lives may laugh.
(*To the gold*) O thou sweet king-killer, and dear
   divorce
'Twixt natural son and sire; thou bright defiler
Of Hymen's purest bed, thou valiant Mars,
Thou ever young, fresh, lov'd, and delicate wooer,
Whose blush doth thaw the consecrated snow
That lies on Dian's lap! thou visible god, 390
That solder'st close impossibilities,
And mak'st them kiss; that speak'st with every
   tongue,
To every purpose: O thou touch of hearts,
Think thy slave man rebels, and by thy virtue
Set them into confounding odds, that beasts
May have the world in empire!
Apemantus.   Would 'twere so,
But not till I am dead. I'll say thou hast gold:
Thou wilt be throng'd to shortly.
Timon.   Throng'd to?
Apemantus.   Ay.
Timon. Thy back, I prithee.
Apemantus.   Live, and love thy misery!
Timon. Long live so, and so die! I am quit. 400
Apemantus. Moe things like men; eat, Timon, and
   abhor them.   *Exit*

Enter Banditti

First Ban. Where should he have this gold? It is

some poor fragment, some slender ort of his re-
mainder: the mere want of gold, and the falling-
from of his friends, drove him into this
melancholy.

Sec. Ban. It is nois'd he hath a mass of treasure.

Third Ban. Let us make the assay upon him; if he
care not for 't, he will supply us easily: if he
covetously reserve it, how shall 's get it?   410

Sec. Ban. True, for he bears it not about him: 'tis
hid.

First Ban. Is not this he?

Banditti. Where?

Sec. Ban. 'Tis his description.

Third Ban. He! I know him.

Banditti. Save thee, Timon.

Timon. Now, thieves?

Banditti. Soldiers, not thieves.

Timon. Both too, and women's sons.   420

Banditti. We are not thieves, but men that much do
want.

Timon. Your greatest want is, you want much of
meat:

Why should you want? Behold, the earth hath
roots:

Within this mile break forth a hundred springs:
The oaks bear mast, the briers scarlet heps,
The bounteous housewife nature, on each bush,
Lays her full mess before you. Want? why want?

First Ban. We cannot live on grass, on berries, water,
As beasts, and birds, and fishes.

Timon. Nor on the beasts themselves, the birds, and
fishes;   430

77

You must eat men. Yet thanks I must you con,
That you are thieves profess'd; that you work not
In holier shapes: for there is boundless theft
In limited professions. Rascal thieves,
Here's gold. Go, suck the subtle blood o' the
    grape,
Till the high fever seethe your blood to froth,
And so 'scape hanging. Trust not the physician,
His antidotes are poison, and he slays
Moe than you rob: take wealth and lives to-
    gether;
Do villainy, do, since you protest to do 't,   440
Like workmen. I'll example you with thievery:
The sun's a thief, and with his great attraction
Robs the vast sea. The moon's an arrant thief,
And her pale fire she snatches from the sun.
The sea's a thief, whose liquid surge resolves
The moon into salt tears. The earth's a thief,
That feeds and breeds by a composture stol'n
From general excrement: each thing's a thief.
The laws, your curb and whip, in their rough
    power
Has uncheck'd theft. Love not yourselves, away,   450
Rob one another, there's more gold, cut throats,
All that you meet are thieves: to Athens go,
Break open shops, nothing can you steal,
But thieves do lose it: steal no less for this
I give you, and gold confound you howsoe'er:
Amen.

Third Ban. Has almost charm'd me from my profession, by persuading me to it.

First Ban. 'Tis in the malice of mankind, that he

thus advises us, not to have us thrive in our   460
mystery.

Sec. Ban. I'll believe him as an enemy, and give
over my trade.

First Ban. Let us first see peace in Athens; there is
no time so miserable but a man may be true.

Exeunt Banditti

Enter Flavius

Flavius. O you gods!
Is yond despis'd and ruinous man my lord?
Full of decay and failing? O monument
And wonder of good deeds, evilly bestow'd!
What an alteration of honour   470
Has desperate want made!
What viler thing upon the earth than friends,
Who can bring noblest minds to basest ends!
How rarely does it meet with this time's guise,
When man was wish'd to love his enemies!
Grant I may ever love, and rather woo
Those that would mischief me than those that do:
Has caught me in his eye, I will present
My honest grief unto him; and, as my lord,
Still serve him with my life. My dearest master! 480
Timon. Away! what art thou?
Flavius.   Have you forgot me, sir?
Timon. Why dost ask that? I have forgot all men.
Then, if thou grant'st thou'rt a man, I have forgot
thee.
Flavius. An honest poor servant of yours.
Timon. Then I know thee not:
I never had honest man about me; ay, all

I kept were knaves, to serve-in meat to villains.
Flavius. The gods are witness,
  Ne'er did poor steward wear a truer grief
  For his undone lord than mine eyes for you.   490
Timon. What, dost thou weep? come nearer, then I
    love thee,
  Because thou art a woman, and disclaim'st
  Flinty mankind; whose eyes do never give
  But thorough lust and laughter. Pity's sleeping:
  Strange times, that weep with laughing, not with
    weeping!
Flavius. I beg of you to know me, good my lord,
  To accept my grief, and, whilst this poor wealth
    lasts,
  To entertain me as your steward still.
Timon. Had I a steward
  So true, so just, and now so comfortable?   500
  It almost turns my dangerous nature mild.
  Let me behold thy face. Surely, this man
  Was born of woman.
  Forgive my general and exceptless rashness,
  You perpetual-sober gods! I do proclaim
  One honest man: mistake me not, but one:
  No more, I pray, and he's a steward.
  How fain would I have hated all mankind,
  And thou redeem'st thyself. But all save thee
  I fell with curses.   510
  Methinks thou art more honest now than wise:
  For, by oppressing and betraying me,
  Thou mightst have sooner got another service:
  For many so arrive at second masters,

Upon their first lord's neck. But tell me true
(For I must ever doubt, though ne'er so sure)
Is not thy kindness subtle, covetous,
If not a usuring kindness, and as rich men deal
    gifts,
Expecting in return twenty for one?
Flavius. No, my most worthy master, in whose breast 520
  Doubt and suspect, alas, are plac'd too late:
  You should have fear'd false times, when you did
    feast:
  Suspect still comes, where an estate is least.
  That which I show, heaven knows, is merely love,
  Duty, and zeal, to your unmatched mind,
  Care of your food and living; and, believe it,
  My most honour'd lord,
  For any benefit that points to me,
  Either in hope, or present, I'ld exchange
  For this one wish, that you had power and wealth 530
  To requite me, by making rich yourself.
Timon. Look thee, 'tis so! Thou singly honest man,
  Here, take: the gods, out of my misery,
  Have sent thee treasure. Go, live rich and happy;
  But thus condition'd: thou shalt build from men:
  Hate all, curse all, show charity to none,
  But let the famish'd flesh slide from the bone
  Ere thou relieve the beggar. Give to dogs
  What thou deniest to men. Let prisons swallow
    'em,
  Debts wither 'em to nothing, be men like blasted
    woods, 540
  And may diseases lick up their false bloods;
  And so farewell, and thrive.

Flavius.   O, let me stay,
  And comfort you, my master.
Timon.   If thou hat'st curses
  Stay not: fly, whilst thou art blest and free:
  Ne'er see thou man, and let me ne'er see thee.
                                    Exeunt severally

Enter Poet and Painter

Painter. As I took note of the place, it cannot be far
  where he abides.
Poet. What's to be thought of him? does the rumour
  hold for true, that he's so full of gold?
Painter. Certain: Alcibiades reports it; Phrynia and
  Timandra had gold of him. He likewise enrich'd
  poor straggling soldiers, with great quantity. 'Tis
  said he gave unto his steward a mighty sum.
Poet. Then this breaking of his has been but a try for
  his friends?   10
Painter. Nothing else: you shall see him a palm in
  Athens again, and flourish with the highest:
  therefore 'tis not amiss we tender our loves to
  him in this suppos'd distress of his: it will show
  honestly in us, and is very likely to load our
  purposes with what they travail for, if it be a just
  and true report that goes of his having.
Poet. What have you now to present unto him?
Painter. Nothing at this time but my visitation: only
  I will promise him an excellent piece.   20

82

Poet. I must serve him so too; tell him of an intent
that's coming toward him.

Painter. Good as the best. Promising is the very air
o' the time; it opens the eyes of expectation: performance is ever the duller for his act; and, but in
the plainer and simpler kind of people, the deed
of saying is quite out of use. To promise is most
courtly and fashionable; performance is a kind of
will or testament which argues a great sickness
in his judgement that makes it.   30

Enter Timon from his cave

Timon. (*aside*) Excellent workman, thou canst not
paint a man so bad as is thyself.

Poet. I am thinking what I shall say I have provided
for him: it must be a personating of himself; a
satire against the softness of prosperity, with a
discovery of the infinite flatteries that follow
youth and opulency.

Timon. (*aside*) Must thou needs stand for a villain
in thine own work? wilt thou whip thine own
faults in other men? Do so, I have gold for thee.   40

Poet. Nay, let's seek him.
Then do we sin against our own estate,
When we may profit meet, and come too late.

Painter. True:
When the day serves, before black-corner'd night,
Find what thou want'st, by free and offer'd light.
Come.

Timon. (*aside*) I'll meet you at the turn. What a
god's gold,
That he is worshipp'd in a baser temple

Than where swine feed! 50
'Tis thou that rigg'st the bark, and plough'st the
 foam,
Settlest admired reverence in a slave;
To thee be worship! and thy saints for aye
Be crown'd with plagues, that thee alone obey!
Fit I meet them. *Coming forward*
Poet. Hail, worthy Timon!
Painter. Our late noble master!
Timon. Have I once liv'd to see two honest men?
Poet. Sir,
 Having often of your open bounty tasted,
 Hearing you were retir'd, your friends fall'n off, 60
 Whose thankless natures (O abhorred spirits!)
 Not all the whips of heaven are large enough—
 What! to you,
 Whose star-like nobleness gave life and influence
 To their whole being? I am rapt, and cannot
 cover
 The monstrous bulk of this ingratitude
 With any size of words.
Timon. Let it go naked, men may see 't the better:
 You that are honest, by being what you are,
 Make them best seen, and known.
Painter. He and myself 70
 Have travail'd in the great shower of your gifts,
 And sweetly felt it.
Timon. Ay, you are honest men.
Painter. We are hither come to offer you our service.
Timon. Most honest men: why, how shall I requite
 you?
 Can you eat roots, and drink cold water? no.

Both. What we can do, we'll do to do you service.

Timon. Ye're honest men, ye've heard that I have
    gold,
  I am sure you have, speak truth, ye're honest
    men.

Painter. So it is said, my noble lord, but therefore
  Came not my friend nor I.   80

Timon. Good honest men! Thou draw'st a counter-
    feit
  Best in all Athens, thou'rt indeed the best,
  Thou counterfeit'st most lively.

Painter.   So, so, my lord.

Timon. E'en so, sir, as I say. And, for thy fiction,
  Why, thy verse swells with stuff so fine and
    smooth
  That thou art even natural in thine art.
  But, for all this, my honest-natur'd friends,
  I must needs say you have a little fault,
  Marry, 'tis not monstrous in you, neither wish I
  You take much pains to mend.

Both.   Beseech your honour 90
  To make it known to us.

Timon.   You'll take it ill.

Both. Most thankfully, my lord.

Timon.   Will you, indeed?

Both. Doubt it not, worthy lord.

Timon. There's never a one of you but trusts a
    knave,
  That mightily deceives you.

Both.   Do we, my lord?

Timon. Ay, and you hear him cog, see him dis-
    semble,

Know his gross patchery, love him, feed him,
Keep in your bosom, yet remain assur'd
That he's a made-up villain.
Painter. I know none such, my lord.
Poet.   Nor I.   100
Timon. Look you, I love you well, I'll give you gold,
  Rid me these villains from your companies;
  Hang them, or stab them, drown them in a
    draught,
  Confound them by some course, and come to me,
  I'll give you gold enough.
Both. Name them, my lord, let's know them.
Timon. You that way, and you this: but two in
    company:
  Each man apart, all single, and alone,
  Yet an arch-villain keeps him company
  If, where thou art, two villains shall not be,   110
  Come not near him. If thou wouldst not reside
  But where one villain is, then him abandon.
  Hence, pack, there's gold, you came for gold, ye
    slaves:
  (*to Painter*) You have work for me; there's pay-
    ment, hence!
  (*to Poet*) You are an alchemist, make gold of
    that:
  Out, rascal dogs!
      Beats them out, and then retires into his cave

        Enter Flavius and two Senators

Flavius. It is vain that you would speak with
    Timon:
  For he is set so only to himself,

That nothing but himself which looks like man
Is friendly with him.
First Sen.   Bring us to his cave.   120
It is our part and promise to the Athenians
To speak with Timon.
Sec. Sen.   At all times alike
Men are not still the same: 'twas time and griefs
That fram'd him thus. Time, with his fairer hand,
Offering the fortunes of his former days,
The former man may make him: bring us to him,
And chance it as it may.
Flavius.   Here is his cave:
Peace and content be here! Lord Timon! Timon!
Look out, and speak to friends: the Athenians
By two of their most reverend senate greet thee: 130
Speak to them, noble Timon.

Timon comes from his cave

Timon. Thou sun, that comforts, burn! Speak, and
     be hang'd:
For each true word, a blister, and each false
Be as a cauterizing to the root o' the tongue,
Consuming it with speaking!
First Sen.   Worthy Timon,—
Timon. Of none but such as you, and you of Timon.
First Sen. The senators of Athens greet thee, Timon.
Timon. I thank them, and would send them back
     the plague,
Could I but catch it for them.
First. Sen.   O, forget
What we are sorry for ourselves in thee.   140
The senators, with one consent of love,

87

Entreat thee back to Athens, who have thought
On special dignities, which vacant lie
For thy best use and wearing.

Sec. Sen.   They confess
Toward thee forgetfulness too general, gross;
Which now the public body, which doth seldom
Play the recanter, feeling in itself
A lack of Timon's aid, hath sense withal
Of it own fall, restraining aid to Timon,   †
And send forth us, to make their sorrow'd render,   150
Together with a recompense more fruitful
Than their offence can weigh down by the dram,
Ay, even such heaps and sums of love and wealth,
As shall to thee blot out what wrongs were theirs,
And write in thee the figures of their love,
Ever to read them thine.

Timon.   You witch me in it:
Surprise me to the very brink of tears:
Lend me a fool's heart, and a woman's eyes,
And I'll beweep these comforts, worthy senators.

First Sen. Therefore, so please thee to return with
     us,   160
And of our Athens, thine and ours, to take
The captainship, thou shalt be met with thanks,
Allow'd with absolute power, and thy good name
Live with authority: so soon we shall drive back
Of Alcibiades the approaches wild,
Who, like a boar to savage, doth root up
His country's peace.

Sec. Sen.   And shakes his threatening sword
Against the walls of Athens.

First Sen.   Therefore, Timon,—

Timon. Well, sir, I will; therefore, I will, sir, thus:
  If Alcibiades kill my countrymen,   170
  Let Alcibiades know this of Timon,
  That Timon cares not. But if he sack fair Athens,
  And take our goodly aged men by the beards,
  Giving our holy virgins to the stain
  Of contumelious, beastly, mad-brain'd war;
  Then let him know, and tell him Timon speaks it,
  In pity of our aged, and our youth,
  I cannot choose but tell him that I care not,
  And let him take 't at worst: for their knives care
      not,
  While you have throats to answer. For myself,   180
  There's not a whittle in the unruly camp,
  But I do prize it at my love before
  The reverend'st throat in Athens. So I leave you
  To the protection of the prosperous gods,
  As thieves to keepers.

Flavius.   Stay not, all's in vain.

Timon. Why, I was writing of my epitaph,
  It will be seen to-morrow. My long sickness
  Of health, and living, now begins to mend,
  And nothing brings me all things. Go, live still,
  Be Alcibiades your plague, you his;   190
  And last so long enough!

First Sen.   We speak in vain.

Timon. But yet I love my country, and am not
  One that rejoices in the common wreck,
  As common bruit doth put it.

First Sen.   That's well spoke.

Timon. Commend me to my loving countrymen,—
First Sen. These words become your lips as they
   pass thorough them.
Sec. Sen. And enter in our ears, like great tri-
   umphers
   In their applauding gates.
Timon.   Commend me to them,
   And tell them, that to ease them of their griefs,
   Their fears of hostile strokes, their aches, losses,   200
   Their pangs of love, with other incident throes
   That nature's fragile vessel doth sustain
   In life's uncertain voyage, I will some kindness
   do them,
   I'll teach them to prevent wild Alcibiades' wrath.
First Sen. (*aside*) I like this well, he will return
   again.
Timon. I have a tree, which grows here in my close,
   That mine own use invites me to cut down,
   And shortly must I fell it. Tell my friends,
   Tell Athens, in the sequence of degree,
   From high to low throughout, that whoso please   210
   To stop affliction, let him take his haste;
   Come hither ere my tree hath felt the axe,
   And hang himself. I pray you, do my greeting.
Flavius. Trouble him no further, thus you still shall
   find him.
Timon. Come not to me again, but say to Athens,
   Timon hath made his everlasting mansion
   Upon the beached verge of the salt flood,
   Whom once a day with his embossed froth
   The turbulent surge shall cover; thither come,

And let my grave-stone be your oracle.
Lips, let sour words go by, and language end:
What is amiss, plague and infection mend!
Graves only be men's works, and death their
    gain;
Sun, hide thy beams; Timon hath done his reign.
                              Retires to his cave
First Sen. His discontents are unremoveably
Coupled to nature.
Sec. Sen. Our hope in him is dead: let us return,
And strain what other means is left unto us
In our dear peril.
First Sen.   It requires swift foot.   *Exeunt*

SCENE II

Before the walls of Athens

Enter two Senators and a Messenger

First Sen. Thou hast painfully discover'd: are his
    files
As full as thy report?
Messenger.   I have spoke the least.
Besides, his expedition promises
Present approach.
Sec. Sen. We stand much hazard, if they bring not
    Timon.
Messenger. I met a courier, one mine ancient
    friend,
Whom, though in general part we were oppos'd,
Yet our old love made a particular force,

91

And made us speak like friends. This man was
   riding
From Alcibiades to Timon's cave,   10
With letters of entreaty, which imported
His fellowship i' the cause against your city,
In part for his sake mov'd.
First Sen.   Here come our brothers.

Enter Senators from Timon

Third Sen. No talk of Timon, nothing of him expect.
The enemies' drum is heard, and fearful scouring
Doth choke the air with dust: in, and prepare;
Ours is the fall, I fear, our foes the snare.

                                   Exeunt

SCENE III

The woods. Timon's cave, and a rude tomb seen

Enter a Soldier, seeking Timon

Soldier. By all description this should be the place.
Who's here? speak, ho! No answer? What is this?
Timon is dead, who hath outstretch'd his span: †
Some beast read this; there does not live a man.
Dead, sure, and this his grave; what's on this
   tomb,
I cannot read; the character I'll take with wax,
Our captain hath in every figure skill;
An ag'd interpreter, though young in days:
Before proud Athens he's set down by this,
Whose fall the mark of his ambition is.   *Exit*   10

SCENE IV

Before the walls of Athens

Trumpets sound. Enter Alcibiades with his powers

Alcibiades. Sound to this coward and lascivious
   town
   Our terrible approach.   *A parley sounded*

Enter Senators upon the walls

Till now you have gone on and fill'd the time
With all licentious measure, making your wills
The scope of justice. Till now, myself and such
As slept within the shadow of your power
Have wander'd with our travers'd arms, and
   breath'd
Our sufferance vainly: now the time is flush,
When crouching marrow in the bearer strong
Cries, of itself, 'No more:' now breathless wrong   10
Shall sit and pant in your great chairs of ease,
And pursy insolence shall break his wind
With fear and horrid flight.
First Sen.   Noble, and young;
When thy first griefs were but a mere conceit,
Ere thou hadst power, or we had cause of fear,
We sent to thee, to give thy rages balm,
To wipe out our ingratitude, with loves
Above their quantity.
Sec. Sen.   So did we woo
Transformed Timon to our city's love
By humble message, and by promis'd means: 20

93

We were not all unkind, nor all deserve
The common stroke of war.

First Sen.   These walls of ours
Were not erected by their hands from whom
You have receiv'd your grief: nor are they such,
That these great towers, trophies, and schools
    should fall
For private faults in them.

Sec. Sen.   Nor are they living
Who were the motives that you first went out;
Shame, that they wanted cunning, in excess
Hath broke their hearts. March, noble lord,
Into our city with thy banners spread: 30
By decimation and a tithed death,
If thy revenges hunger for that food
Which nature loathes, take thou the destin'd
    tenth,
And by the hazard of the spotted die
Let die the spotted.

First Sen.   All have not offended:
For those that were, it is not square to take,
On those that are, revenge: crimes, like lands
Are not inherited; then, dear countryman,
Bring in thy ranks, but leave without thy rage,
Spare thy Athenian cradle, and those kin   40
Which in the bluster of thy wrath must fall
With those that have offended; like a shepherd,
Approach the fold, and cull the infected forth,
But kill not all together.

Sec. Sen.   What thou wilt,
Thou rather shalt enforce it with thy smile,
Than hew to 't with thy sword.

94

First Sen.   Set but thy foot
   Against our rampir'd gates, and they shall ope:
   So thou wilt send thy gentle heart before,
   To say thou'lt enter friendly.
Sec. Sen.   Throw thy glove,
   Or any token of thine honour else,   50
   That thou wilt use the wars as thy redress,
   And not as our confusion; all thy powers
   Shall make their harbour in our town, till we
   Have seal'd thy full desire.
Alcibiades.   Then there's my glove,
   Descend, and open your uncharged ports:
   Those enemies of Timon's, and mine own,
   Whom you yourselves shall set out for reproof,
   Fall, and no more: and, to atone your fears
   With my more noble meaning, not a man
   Shall pass his quarter, or offend the stream   60
   Of regular justice in your city's bounds,
   But shall be render'd to your public laws
   At heaviest answer.
Both.   'Tis most nobly spoken.
Alcibiades. Descend, and keep your words.
     The Senators descend, and open the gates

       Enter a Messenger

Messenger. My noble general, Timon is dead,
   Entomb'd upon the very hem o' the sea,
   And on his grave-stone this insculpture, which
   With wax I brought away; whose soft impression
   Interprets for my poor ignorance.
Alcibiades. (*reads*)

'Here lies a wretched corse, of wretched soul   †
bereft,   70
Seek not my name: a plague consume you,
wicked caitiffs left!'
'Here lie I, Timon; who, alive, all living men did
hate,
Pass by, and curse thy fill, but pass and stay not
here thy gait.'
These well express in thee thy latter spirits:
Though thou abhorr'dst in us our human griefs,
Scorn'dst our brain's flow, and those our droplets,
which
From niggard nature fall; yet rich conceit
Taught thee to make vast Neptune weep for aye
On thy low grave, on faults forgiven. Dead
Is noble Timon, of whose memory   80
Hereafter more. Bring me into your city,
And I will use the olive, with my sword:
Make war breed peace; make peace stint war;
make each
Prescribe to other, as each other's leech.
Let our drums strike.   *Exeunt*

Notes

THE text of *Timon* is clearly extremely corrupt, and has been the happy hunting ground of the emenders. To give the emendations proposed at all in full would extend the notes to a quite disproportionate length. I have contented myself therefore with including in the text a small number of the more generally accepted emendations, and commenting on a certain number of other dubious passages in the notes. There remain therefore a large number of passages which are certainly difficult and probably corrupt, but of which the cure is so uncertain that it seems better left to the taste of the individual reader. The more one studies the play the more one comes to feel that many passages are not so much 'corrupt' in the ordinary sense, as simply unfinished rough drafts that were to have been worked over. And if that is so, emendation is idle.

I. i. 49. *wide sea of wax*. Many conjectures, none of them carrying much conviction ('vice,' 'tax,' 'man,' 'wast').

I. i. 89. *sit*; so F. The required sense is clear, 'slip' or 'sink,' which have both been suggested, but neither is graphically easy.

I. i. 131–33. The reading given is that of F. There has

been much conjecture. Some sort of sense is produced by taking *Timon* as vocative, so that the old Athenian means that the man is honest, but that is all he will be. I suspect the corruption, if any, to lie in *Timon*.

I. i. 241. *no angry wit.* An unsolved crux. Just possibly *That I had no angry wit to be angry with a lord.*

I. ii. 51. *notes*; F. *noates.* If the reading is to be retained, '*notes*' must be something seen, not heard, *i.e.* must be used in the sense of the Latin *notæ*; but this is not satisfactory.

I. ii. 137. *Like madness . . .* ; *i.e.* 'the glory of this life is *as much* madness as this pomp is when compared to . . .'

I. ii. 252. *in paper.* The explanation 'in paper securities' is unsatisfactory, and there is probably corruption.

II. i. 10. *able.* Vaguely feeble, and probably corrupt: many conjectures. [But *cf. 2 Henry IV*, I. i. 43.]

II. ii. 172. *wasteful cock.* The conjecturers have had a field day over these two words; Pope shut his eyes and said firmly '*lonely room*,' others, less heroic, said '*wasteful nook*,' '*wakeful couch*,' and '*wakeful cot*'; another '*wakeful cock*,' though why the cock should be wakeful, or why Flavius should go to him to pour out his sorrows is not explained; another '*wasteful cock-loft*,' though why Flavius should go to the cock-loft and why it is wasteful is not explained. The only sane hope seems to be to keep as close as may be to the text and assume that Flavius is saying that he wept in the same way as the wasteful cocks were weeping spilth of wine. If there is corruption I would sooner look for it in '*retir'd*': the sense needed is 'made myself like.'

III. i. 49. *And we alive that liv'd; i.e.* 'in so short a

time'; this at least is the accepted explanation, though I cannot feel it wholly adequate.

III. ii. 12, 25, 39, 41. *so many,* and *fifty five hundred.* All very obscure: even if the second stranger did not know the sum, it is odd that Servilius should use so vague a term when Flaminius in the preceding scene has been precise: and *fifty five hundred talents* is too extravagant to be even 'humorous hyperbole,' apart from not being a round sum. We might do something with it by reading '*five-fifty-a hundred-talents.*' But much conjecture has done little but darken counsel.

III. iii. 12. *Thrive.* Not satisfactory: but the many conjectures (*Three, Tried, Shriv'd, Thrice,* etc.) are little more so.

III. iv. 113. *Sempronius: all:* F reads Sempronius Vllorxa: *All.* One of the most famous Shakespearean cruxes, but luckily also one of the least important. Is *Vllorxa* perhaps a misreading of *Villains,* written above *rascals* in the next line as a correction, misread and transferred to the line above?

III. v. 22. *behoove;* thus F. Usually emended to *behave.*

IV. iii. 185. *who all . . . ; the* should probably be *thy;* and thus the emendation either of *who* to *whom,* or of *do* to *doth,* will give sense.

V. i. 149. *fall;* so F. We should perhaps read *fail* or *fault.*

V. iii. 3–4. *Timon is dead,* etc. There are two schools of commentators, (*a*) those who take this line and the next as Timon's epitaph, (*b*) those who take them to be a comment of the soldier. (*a*) are in difficulties to explain first where the inscription is, since it is apparently not on the tomb, and second why the soldier can read this and not the inscription on the tomb; (*b*) are in difficulties to explain what the second line means, and should also be troubled by the intrusive couplet. The scene is hardly important enough to worry about, but I suggest that most of the difficulties would be met by supposing that we have here two different versions of the scene of which the first was not adequately cancelled. In the first the soldier could read, and the couplet was Timon's epitaph, appropriate enough; and the scene was to have consisted of lines 1–4, together with an announcement by the soldier that he would carry the news to his captain. In the second version the soldier could not read, and lines 3 and 4 were to be omitted altogether. Timon's epitaph does not then come till the last scene.

V. iv. 70. Here again it is hard to believe that all four lines were intended to stand. Either of the two couplets could stand by itself.

Glossary

MANY words and phrases in Shakespeare require glossing, not because they are in themselves unfamiliar, but for the opposite reason, that Shakespeare uses in their Elizabethan and unfamiliar sense a large number of words which seem so familiar that there is no incentive to look for them in the glossary. It is hoped that a glossary arranged as below will make it easy to see at a glance what words and phrases in any particular scene require elucidation. A number of phrases are glossed by what seems to be, in their context, the modern equivalent rather than by lexicographical glosses on the words which compose them.

Act First

SCENE I

line
- 10 BREATH'D, trained
- 12 PASSES, surpasses
- 15 TOUCH THE ESTIMATE, rise to the price
- 19 WATER, (*as in 'diamond of the first water'*)
- 28 UPON THE HEELS OF MY PRESENTMENT, as soon as I have presented it to Timon (*as a potential patron*)
- 39 ARTIFICIAL STRIFE, art competing with nature

line
- 43 MOE, more (*the regular Eliz. form for the plural*)
- 59 PROPERTIES, appropriates
  HIS LOVE AND TENDANCE, love and attend on him
- 60 GLASS-FAC'D, reflecting as a mirror
- 74 TO SCOPE, appositely
- 92 MORAL, allegorical
- 101 PERIODS, puts the full stop to
- 129 HER RESORT, resorting to her

Act I Sc. i—*continued*

line

135 PRECEDENT, once-experi-
enced

170 UNCLEW, exhaust re-
sources; (*met. from* un-
winding a ball of wool)

line

175 WELL MOCK'D, clever flattery!

212 APPREHENSION, interpreta-
tion

257 ACHES, *disyllable*

282 OPPOSITE, antagonistic

SCENE II

32 APPERIL, peril

53 IN HEART, 'prosit!'

72 DICH, *contr. of* do it you

117 MUCH! *ironical*

138 SHOWS TO, appears in com-
parison with

144–145 THAT BEARS . . . GIFT;
that has not once been
rejected by his friends

158 IDLE, trifling

168 FOR HIS MIND, as a result
of what he has been
minded to do

175 ADVANCE, raise in dignity

190 PRESENTS, ? those who
bring them (*cf.* l. 196)

206 LAND'S PUT TO THEIR
BOOKS, is (as it were)
mortgaged

210 SUCH, *sc.* friends

223 TELL, reckon
CALL TO, call on

240 COIL, ado

241 BECKS, bows

Act Second

SCENE I

22 FRACTED, dishonoured

30 HIS, its

SCENE II

8 ROUND, blunt

120 STONES, testicles

220 FRACTIONS, disjointed re-
marks

Act Third

SCENE I

45 SOLIDARES, small coins
(*denomination uncer-
tain*)

SCENE IV

line   *line*

42 IN A CLOUD, moodily

SCENE V

21 UNNOTED, undemonstrative
22 BEHOOVE, ? control
24 UNDERGO, undertake
   STRICT, strained
54 GUST, outburst (*or* ? relish)
55 BY MERCY, in the eyes of a
   merciful judge
61 A SUFFICIENT BRIBER FOR,
   sufficient to purchase

73 HIS DRINK DANGEROUS, he is
   dangerous in drink
102 TO SWELL OUR SPIRIT, to
    work ourselves into
    higher passion
103 PRESENTLY, immediately
115 LAY FOR, plan to win

SCENE VI

4 TIRING, feeding (*met.*
  from falconry)

103 MINUTE-JACKS, ? figures
    on a clock, *i.e.* time
    servers

Act Fourth

SCENE I

12 PILL, pillage
14 LIN'D, padded

18 MYSTERIES, occupations
   (métiers)
25 LIBERTY, licence

SCENE III

5 IS DIVIDANT, distinguish
  them
12 LARDS, fattens
   ROTHER, OX
16 GRISE, step
18 OBLIQUY, obliquity
27 VOTARIST, gold-worshipper
38 WAPPER'D, worn out (see
   N.E.D.)
85 SALT, salacious
87 TUB-FAST, sweating-cure

116 WINDOW-BARS, lattice-work
    in front of bodice
122 OBJECTS, objects calculated
    to excite pity
135 OATHABLE, fit to take oath
155 QUILLETS, quibbles (*quid-*
    libet)
    FLAMEN, priest
160 FROM, irrespective of
184 HYPERION, the sun-god
222 CHAMBERLAIN, valet

Act IV   Sc. iii—*continued*

line

224 PAGE THY HEELS, follow like pages
226 CAUDLE, give a pick-me-up
252 SWATH, swaddling-clothes
342 GERMAN, kin
393 TOUCH, touchstone
403 ORT, fragment

line

425 MAST, acorns (*as food for pigs*)
    HEPS, hips (berries)
431 CON THANKS, be grateful to
461 MYSTERY, *see* IV. i. 18
500 COMFORTABLE, consoling

Act Fifth

SCENE I

96 COG, cheat
97 PATCHERY, trickery
140 IN, with regard to
150 RENDER, surrender *or* rendering of account

181 WHITTLE, clasp-knife
206 CLOSE, enclosure
218 HIS, its
229 DEAR, extreme

SCENE IV

5 SCOPE, bounds
7 TRAVERS'D, folded
8 FLUSH, ripe
12 PURSY, short-winded
25 TROPHIES, monuments
   SCHOOLS, *i.e. of philosophy*
36 SQUARE, fair
47 RAMPIR'D, fortified

55 UNCHARGED PORTS, unassailed gates
58 ATONE, calm
60 PASS HIS QUARTER, break the 'quarter' that has been given
77 RICH CONCEIT, fertile imagination

This book may be kept

FOURTEEN DAYS

A fine will be charged for each day the book is kept overtime.

GAYLORD 142